Fix-It and Forget-It®
SIMPLE & SATISFYING

Fix-It and Forget-It® Simple & Satisfying

Weeknight Dinners for Your Slow Cooker or Instant Pot

HOPE COMERFORD
Photos by Bonnie Matthews

New York, New York

Copyright © 2025 by Good Books

Photos by Bonnie Matthews

All rights reserved. No part of this book may be reproduced in any manner without the express written consent of the publisher, except in the case of brief excerpts in critical reviews or articles. All inquiries should be addressed to Good Books, 307 West 36th Street, 11th Floor, New York, NY 10018.

Good Books books may be purchased in bulk at special discounts for sales promotion, corporate gifts, fund-raising, or educational purposes. Special editions can also be created to specifications. For details, contact the Special Sales Department, Good Books, 307 West 36th Street, 11th Floor, New York, NY 10018 or info@skyhorsepublishing.com.

Good Books is an imprint of Skyhorse Publishing, Inc.®, a Delaware corporation.

Visit our website at www.goodbooks.com.

10 9 8 7 6 5 4 3 2 1

Library of Congress Cataloging-in-Publication Data is available on file.

Cover design by Kai Texel
Cover photo by Bonnie Matthews

Print ISBN: 978-1-68099-961-7
Ebook ISBN: 978-1-68099-971-6

Printed in China

Contents

Welcome to *Fix-It and Forget-It Simple & Satisfying* ❧ 1
    Choosing a Slow Cooker ❧ 1
    Get to Know Your Slow Cooker ❧ 3
    Slow-Cooker Tips and Tricks and Other Things You May Not Know ❧ 4
    What Is an Instant Pot? ❧ 7
    Getting Started with Your Instant Pot ❧ 7
    Instant Pot Tips and Tricks and Other Things You May Not Know ❧ 9
    Instant Pot Accessories ❧ 12

❧ Recipes ❧

Breakfast for Dinner ❧ 13

Soups, Stews, Chilis & Chowders ❧ 39
    Chicken ❧ 41
    Pork ❧ 51
    Beef ❧ 63
    Meatless ❧ 73

Main Dishes ❧ 87
    Chicken & Turkey ❧ 89
    Pork ❧ 113
    Beef ❧ 133
    Meatless & Seafood ❧ 155

Sides ❧ 167

Desserts ❧ 191

Metric Equivalent Measurements ❧ 214
Recipe & Ingredient Index ❧ 215
About the Author ❧ 226

Welcome to Fix-It and Forget-It Simple & Satisfying!

Whether your weeknights are busy or laid-back, Fix-It and Forget-It has got you covered! With 127 easy to prepare, make, and serve Instant Pot or slow-cooker recipes, weeknight meals will be a breeze. You won't have to hunt through the grocery store to find "odd" ingredients either because most of the recipes in this book contain items you might even already have in your pantry, cupboards, or freezer.

Make breakfast simple with recipes like Fiesta Hashbrowns or Cinnamon French Toast Casserole. Conquer the dinner rush with recipes like Tuscan Beef Stew, Flavorful French Dip, Tortellini with Broccoli, Barbecued Brisket, and more! Satisfy that sweet tooth with desserts like S'mores Lava Cake, Buttery Rice Pudding, or Strawberry Shortcake.

Whatever you choose to make from this cookbook, know that all the recipes came from home cooks just like you! Your mealtimes should be simple and satisfying, and that's just what this book is here for. So start making that grocery list and get cooking!

Choosing a Slow Cooker

Not All Slow Cookers Are Created Equal . . . or Work Equally as Well for Everyone!

Those of us who use slow cookers frequently know we have our own preferences when it comes to which slow cooker we choose to use. For instance, I love my programmable slow cooker, but there are many programmable slow cookers I've tried that I've strongly disliked. Why? Because some go by increments of 15 or 30 minutes and some go by 4, 6, 8, or 10 hours. I dislike those restrictions, but I have family and friends who don't mind them at all! I am also pretty brand loyal when it comes to my manual slow cookers because I've had great success with those and have had unsuccessful moments with slow cookers of other brands. So, which slow cooker(s) is/are best for your household?

It really depends on how many people you're feeding and if you're gone for long periods of time. Here are my recommendations:

For 2–3 person household	3–5 quart slow cooker
For 4–5 person household	5–6 quart slow cooker
For 6+ person household	6½–7 quart slow cooker

Large Slow-Cooker Advantages/Disadvantages

Advantages:
- You can fit a loaf pan or a baking dish into a 6- or 7-quart, depending on the shape of your cooker. That allows you to make bread or cakes, or even smaller quantities of main dishes. (Take your favorite baking dish and loaf pan along when you shop for a cooker to make sure they'll fit inside.)
- You can feed large groups of people, or make larger quantities of food, allowing for leftovers, or meals, to freeze.

Disadvantages:
- They take up more storage room.
- They don't fit as neatly into a dishwasher.
- If your crock isn't ⅔–¾ full, you may burn your food.

Small Slow-Cooker Advantages/Disadvantages

Advantages:
- They're great for lots of appetizers, for serving hot drinks, for baking cakes straight in the crock, and for dorm rooms or apartments.
- Great option for making recipes of smaller quantities.

Disadvantages:
- Food in smaller quantities tends to cook more quickly than larger amounts. So keep an eye on it.
- Chances are, you won't have many leftovers. So, if you like to have leftovers, a smaller slow cooker may not be a good option for you.

My Recommendation

Have at least two slow cookers; one around 3 to 4 quarts and one 6 quarts or larger. A third would be a huge bonus (and a great advantage to your cooking repertoire!). The advantage of having at least a couple is you can make a larger variety of recipes. Also, you can make at least two or three dishes at once for a whole meal.

Manual vs. Programmable

If you are gone for only six to eight hours a day, a manual slow cooker might be just fine for you. If you are gone for more than eight hours during the day, I would highly recommend purchasing a programmable slow cooker that will switch to warm when the cook time you set is up. It will allow you to cook a wider variety of recipes.

The two I use most frequently are my 4-quart manual slow cooker and my 6½-quart programmable slow cooker. I like that I can make smaller portions in my 4-quart slow cooker on days I don't need or want leftovers, but I also love how my 6½-quart slow cooker can accommodate whole chickens, turkey breasts, hams, or big batches of soups. I use them both often.

Get to Know Your Slow Cooker . . .

Plan a little time to get acquainted with your slow cooker. Each slow cooker has its own personality—just like your oven (and your car). Plus, many new slow cookers cook hotter and faster than earlier models. I think that with all of the concern for food safety, the slow-cooker manufacturers have amped up their settings so that "High," "Low," and "Warm" are all higher temperatures than in the older models. That means they cook hotter—and therefore, faster—than the first slow cookers. The beauty of these little machines is that they're supposed to cook low and slow. We count on that when we flip the switch in the morning before we leave the house for ten hours or so. So, because none of us knows what kind of temperament our slow cooker has until we try it out, nor how hot it cooks—don't assume anything. Save yourself a disappointment and make the first recipe in your new slow cooker on a day when you're at home. Cook it for the shortest amount of time the recipe calls for. Then, check the food to see if it's done. Or if you start smelling food that seems to be finished, turn off the cooker and rescue your food.

Also, all slow cookers seem to have a "hot spot," which is of great importance to know, especially when baking with your slow cooker. This spot may tend to burn food in that area if you're not careful. If you're baking directly in your slow cooker, I recommend covering the "hot spot" with some foil.

Take Notes . . .

Don't be afraid to make notes in your cookbook. It's yours! Chances are, it will eventually get passed down to someone in your family and they will love and appreciate all of your musings. Take note of which slow cooker you used and exactly how long it took to cook the recipe. The next time you make it, you won't need to try to remember. Apply what you learned to the next recipes you make in your cooker. If another recipe says it needs to cook 7–9 hours, and you've discovered your slow cooker cooks on the faster side, cook that recipe for 6–6½ hours and then check it. You can always cook a recipe longer—but you can't reverse things if it's overdone.

Get Creative . . .

If you know your morning is going to be hectic, prepare everything the night before, take it out so the crock warms up to room temperature when you first get up in the morning, then plug it in and turn it on as you're leaving the house.

If you want to make something that has a short cook time and you're going to be gone longer than that, cook it the night before and refrigerate it for the next day. Warm it up when you get home. Or, cook those recipes on the weekend when you know you'll be home and eat them later in the week.

Slow-Cooker Tips and Tricks and Other Things You May Not Know

- Slow cookers tend to work best when they're ⅔ to ¾ of the way full. You may need to increase the cooking time if you've exceeded that amount, or reduce it if you've put in less than that. If you're going to exceed that limit, it would be best to reduce the recipe, or split it between two slow cookers. (Remember how I suggested owning at least two or three slow cookers?)
- Keep your veggies on the bottom. That puts them in more direct contact with the heat. The fuller your slow cooker, the longer it will take its contents to cook. Also, the more densely packed the cooker's contents are, the longer they will take to cook. And finally, the larger the chunks of meat or vegetables, the more time they will need to cook.
- Keep the lid on! Every time you take a peek, you lose 20 minutes of cooking time. Please take this into consideration each time you lift the lid! I know, some of you can't help yourselves and are going to lift anyway. Just don't forget to tack on 20 minutes to your cook time for each time you peeked!

- Sometimes it's beneficial to remove the lid. If you'd like your dish to thicken a bit, take the lid off during the last half hour to hour of cooking time.
- If you have a big slow cooker (7- to 8-quart), you can cook a small batch in it by putting the recipe ingredients into an oven-safe baking dish or baking pan and then placing that into the cooker's crock. First, put a trivet or some metal jar rings on the bottom of the crock, and then set your dish or pan on top of them. Or a loaf pan may "hook onto" the top ridges of the crock belonging to a large oval cooker and hang there straight and securely, "baking" a cake or quick bread. Cover the cooker and flip it on.
- The outside of your slow cooker will be hot! Please remember to keep it out of reach of children and keep that in mind for yourself as well!
- Get yourself a quick-read meat thermometer and use it! This helps remove the question of whether or not your meat is fully cooked, and helps prevent you from overcooking your meat as well.
  - Internal Cooking Temperatures: Beef—125–130°F (rare); 140–145°F (medium); 160°F (well-done)
  - Pork—140–145°F (rare); 145–150°F (medium); 160°F (well-done)
  - Turkey and Chicken—165°F
  - Frozen meat: The basic rule of thumb is, don't put frozen meat into the slow cooker. The meat does not reach the proper internal temperature in time. This especially applies to thick cuts of meat! Proceed with caution!
- Add fresh herbs 10 minutes before the end of the cooking time to maximize their flavor.
- If your recipe calls for cooked pasta, add it 10 minutes before the end of the cooking time if the cooker is on High; 30 minutes before the end of the cooking time if it's on Low. Then the pasta won't get mushy.
- If your recipe calls for sour cream or cream, stir it in 5 minutes before the end of the cooking time. You want it to heat but not boil or simmer.
- Approximate Slow-Cooker Temperatures (Remember, each slow cooker is different):
  - High—212–300°F
  - Low—170–200°F
  - Simmer—185°F
  - Warm—165°F
- Cooked beans freeze well. Store them in freezer bags (squeeze the air out first) or freezer boxes. Cooked and dried bean measurements:
  - 16-oz. can, drained = about 1¾ cups beans
  - 19-oz. can, drained = about 2 cups beans
  - 1 lb. dried beans (about 2½ cups) = 5 cups cooked beans

What Is an Instant Pot?

In short, an Instant Pot is a digital pressure cooker that also has multiple other functions. Not only can it be used as a pressure cooker, but depending on which model Instant Pot you have, you can set it to do things like sauté, cook rice, grains, porridge, soup/stew, beans/chili, porridge, meat, poultry, cake, eggs, yogurt. You can use the Instant Pot to steam or slow cook or even set it manually. Because the Instant Pot has so many functions, it takes away the need for multiple appliances on your counter and allows you to use fewer pots and pans.

Getting Started with Your Instant Pot

Get to Know Your Instant Pot . . .

The very first thing most Instant Pot owners do is called the water test. It helps you get to know your Instant Pot a bit, familiarizes you with it, and might even take a bit of your apprehension away (because if you're anything like me, I was scared to death to use it).

Step 1: Plug in your Instant Pot. This may seem obvious to some, but when we're nervous about using a new appliance, sometimes we forget things like this.

Step 2: Make sure the inner pot is inserted in the cooker. You should *never* attempt to cook anything in your device without the inner pot, or you will ruin your Instant Pot. Food should never come into contact with the actual housing unit.

Step 3: The inner pot has lines for each cup. Fill the inner pot with water until it reaches the 3-cup line.

Step 4: Check the sealing ring to be sure it's secure and in place. You should not be able to move it around. If it's not in place properly, you may experience issues with the pot letting out a lot of steam while cooking, or not coming to pressure.

Step 5: Seal the lid. There is an arrow on the lid between "open" and "close." There is also an arrow on the top of the base of the Instant Pot between a picture of a locked lock and an unlocked lock. Line those arrows up, then turn the lid toward the picture of the lock (left). You will hear a noise that will indicate the lid is locked. If you do not hear a noise, it's not locked. Try it again.

Step 6: *Always* check to see if the steam valve on top of the lid is turned to "sealing." If it's not on "sealing" and is on "venting," it will not be able to come to pressure.

Step 7: Press the "Steam" button and use the +/− arrow to set it to 2 minutes. Once it's at the desired time, you don't need to press anything else. In a few seconds, the Instant Pot will begin all on its own. For those of us with digital slow cookers, we have a tendency to look for the "start" button, but there isn't one on the Instant Pot.

Step 8: Now you wait for the "magic" to happen! The cooking will begin once the device comes to pressure. This can take anywhere from 5 to 30 minutes, in my experience. Then, you will see the countdown happen (from the time you set it for). After that, the Instant Pot will beep, which means your meal is done!

Step 9: Your Instant Pot will now automatically switch to "warm" and begin a count of how many minutes it's been on warm. The next part is where you either wait for the NPR, or natural pressure release (the pressure releases on its own), or do what's called a QR, or quick release (you manually release the pressure). Which method you choose depends on what you're cooking, but in this case, you can choose either, because it's just water. For NPR, you will wait for the lever to move all the way back over to "venting" and watch the pinion (float valve) next to the lever. It will be flush with the lid when at full pressure and will drop when the pressure is done releasing. If you choose QR, be very careful not to have your hands over the vent, as the steam is very hot and you can burn yourself.

The Three Most Important Buttons You Need to Know About

You will find the majority of recipes will use the following three buttons:

Manual/Pressure Cook: Some older models tend to say "Manual," and the newer models seem to say "Pressure Cook." They mean the same thing. From here, you use the +/- button to change the cook time. After several seconds, the Instant Pot will begin its process. The exact name of this button will vary on your model of Instant Pot.

Sauté: Many recipes will have you sauté vegetables, or brown meat before beginning the pressure cooking process. For this setting, you will not use the lid of the Instant Pot.

Keep Warm/Cancel: This may just be the most important button on the Instant Pot. When you forget to use the +/- buttons to change the time for a recipe, or you press a wrong button, you can hit "keep warm/cancel" and it will turn your Instant Pot off for you.

What Do All the Buttons Do?

With so many buttons, it's hard to remember what each one does or means. You can use this as a quick guide in a pinch.

Soup/Broth. This button cooks at high pressure for 30 minutes. It can be adjusted using the +/- buttons to cook more, for 40 minutes, or less, for 20 minutes.

Meat/Stew. This button cooks at high pressure for 35 minutes. It can be adjusted using the +/- buttons to cook more, for 45 minutes, or less, for 20 minutes.

Bean/Chili. This button cooks at high pressure for 30 minutes. It can be adjusted using the +/- buttons to cook more, for 40 minutes, or less, for 25 minutes.

Poultry. This button cooks at high pressure for 15 minutes. It can be adjusted using the +/- buttons to cook more, for 30 minutes, or less, for 5 minutes.

Rice. This button cooks at low pressure and is the only fully automatic program. It is for cooking white rice and will automatically adjust the cooking time depending on the amount of water and rice in the cooking pot.

Multigrain. This button cooks at high pressure for 40 minutes. It can be adjusted using the +/- buttons to cook more, for 45 minutes of warm water soaking time and 60 minutes pressure cooking time, or less, for 20 minutes.

Porridge. This button cooks at high pressure for 20 minutes. It can be adjusted using the +/- buttons to cook more, for 30 minutes, or less, for 15 minutes.

Steam. This button cooks at high pressure for 10 minutes. It can be adjusted using the +/- buttons to cook more, for 15 minutes, or less, for 3 minutes. Always use a rack or steamer basket with this function, because it heats at full power continuously while it's coming to pressure, and you do not want food in direct contact with the bottom of the pressure cooking pot or it will burn. Once it reaches pressure, the steam button regulates pressure by cycling on and off, similar to the other pressure buttons.

Less | Normal | More. Adjust between the *Less | Normal | More* settings by pressing the same cooking function button repeatedly until you get to the desired setting. (Older versions use the *Adjust* button.)

+/- Buttons. Adjust the cook time up [+] or down [-]. (On newer models, you can also press and hold [-] or [+] for 3 seconds to turn sound OFF or ON.)

Cake. This button cooks at high pressure for 30 minutes. It can be adjusted using the +/- buttons to cook more, for 40 minutes, or less, for 25 minutes.

Egg. This button cooks at high pressure for 5 minutes. It can be adjusted using the +/- buttons to cook more, for 6 minutes, or less, for 4 minutes.

Instant Pot Tips and Tricks and Other Things You May Not Know

- Never attempt to cook directly in the Instant Pot without the inner pot!
- Once you set the time, you can walk away. It will show the time you set it to, then will change to the word "on" while the pressure builds. Once the Instant Pot has come to pressure, you will once again see the time you set it for. It will count down from there.

- Always make sure the sealing ring is securely in place. If it shows signs of wear or tear, it needs to be replaced.
- Have a sealing ring for savory recipes and a separate sealing ring for sweet recipes. Many people report their desserts tasting like a roast (or another savory food) if they try to use the same sealing ring for all recipes.
- The stainless steel rack (trivet) the Instant Pot comes with can be used to keep food from being completely submerged in liquid, like baked potatoes or ground beef. It can also be used to set another pot on, for pot-in-pot cooking.
- If you use warm or hot liquid instead of cold liquid, you may need to adjust the cooking time, or the food may not come out done.
- Always double-check to see that the valve on the lid is set to "sealing" and not "venting" when you first lock the lid. This will save you from the Instant Pot not coming to pressure.
- Use Natural Pressure Release for tougher cuts of meat, recipes with high starch (like rice or grains), and recipes with a high volume of liquid. This means you let the Instant Pot naturally release pressure. The little bobbin will fall once pressure is released completely.
- Use Quick Release for more delicate cuts of meat, such as seafood and chicken breasts, and for steaming vegetables. This means you manually turn the vent (being careful not to put your hand over the vent) to release the pressure. The little bobbin will fall once pressure is released completely.
- Make sure there is a clear pathway for the steam to release. The last thing you want is to ruin the bottom of your cupboards with all that steam.
- You *must* use liquid in the Instant Pot. The *minimum* amount of liquid you should have in the inner pot is ½ cup, but most recipes work best with at least 1 cup.
- Do *not* overfill the Instant Pot! It should only be ½ full for rice or beans (food that expands greatly when cooked) or ⅔ of the way full for almost everything else. Do not fill it to the max fill line.
- In this book, the Cook Time *does not* take into account the amount of time it will take the Instant Pot to come to pressure, or the amount of time it will take the Instant Pot to release pressure. Be aware of this when choosing a recipe to make.
- If the Instant Pot is not coming to pressure, it's usually because the sealing ring is not on properly, or the vent is not set to "sealing."
- The more liquid, or the colder the ingredients, the longer it will take for the Instant Pot to come to pressure.
- Always make sure that the Instant Pot is dry before inserting the inner pot, and make sure the inner pot is dry before inserting it into the Instant Pot.

- Use a binder clip to hold the inner pot tight against the outer pot when sautéing and stirring. This will keep the pot from "spinning" in the base.
- Doubling a recipe does not change the cook time, but instead it will take longer to come up to pressure.
- You do not always need to double the liquid when doubling a recipe. Depending on what you're making, more liquid may make the food too watery. Use your best judgment.
- When using the slow-cooker function, use the following chart:

Slow Cooker	Instant Pot
Warm	Less or Low
Low	Normal or Medium
High	More or High

Instant Pot Accessories

Most Instant Pots come with a stainless steel trivet. Below, you will find a list of common accessories that are frequently used in most Fix-It and Forget-It Instant Pot cookbooks. Most of these accessories can be purchased in-store or online.

- Steamer basket—stainless steel or silicone
- 7-inch nonstick or silicone springform or cake pan
- 7-inch nonstick Bundt pan
- Sling or trivet with handles
- 1½-quart round baking dish
- Silicon egg molds

Breakfast for Dinner

Egg Bites

Hope Comerford, Clinton Township, MI

Makes 14 mini quiches
Prep. Time: 15 minutes ❦ Cooking Time: 11 minutes ❦ Cooling Time: 5 minutes

2 tsp. olive oil
½ green bell pepper, diced
¼ cup finely chopped broccoli florets
½ small onion, diced
5 oz. fresh spinach
8 eggs
¼ cup nonfat milk
3 drops hot sauce, *optional*
⅓ cup shredded reduced-fat cheddar cheese
1 cup water

1. In a small pan on the stove, heat the olive oil over medium-high heat. Sauté the bell pepper, broccoli, and onion for about 8 minutes. Add the spinach and continue to cook until wilted.

2. Spray 2 egg molds with nonstick cooking spray. Divide the cooked vegetables evenly between the egg bite mold cups.

3. In a bowl, whisk the eggs, milk, and hot sauce (if using). Divide this evenly between the egg bite mold cups, or until each cup is ⅔ of the way full.

4. Evenly divide the shredded cheese between the cups. Cover them tightly with foil.

5. Pour the water into the inner pot of the Instant Pot. Place the trivet on top, then place the 2 filled egg bite molds on top of the trivet, the top one stacked staggered on top of the one below.

6. Secure the lid and set the vent to sealing.

7. Manually set the cook time for 11 minutes on high pressure.

8. When the cook time is up, let the pressure release naturally for 5 minutes, then manually release the remaining pressure.

9. When the pin drops, remove the lid and carefully lift the trivet and molds out with oven mitts.

10. Place the molds on a wire rack and uncover. Let cool for about 5 minutes, then pop them out onto a plate or serving platter.

Serving suggestion:
Serve alongside your favorite healthy bread and a bowl of fruit.

Breakfast for Dinner

Easy Quiche

Becky Bontrager Horst, Goshen, IN

Makes 6 servings, 1 slice per serving
Prep. Time: 15 minutes   Cooking Time: 25 minutes

1 cup water

¼ cup chopped onion

¼ cup chopped mushrooms, *optional*

3 oz. shredded reduced-fat cheddar cheese

2 Tbsp. bacon bits, chopped ham, or browned sausage

4 eggs

¼ tsp. salt

1½ cups nonfat milk

½ cup whole wheat flour

1 Tbsp. trans-fat–free soft margarine

1. Pour the water into the inner pot of the Instant Pot and place the steaming rack inside.

2. Spray a 7-inch round baking pan with nonstick cooking spray.

3. Sprinkle the onion, mushrooms, shredded cheddar, and meat in the cake pan.

4. In a medium bowl, combine the remaining ingredients. Pour them over the meat and vegetables.

5. Place the baking pan onto the steaming rack, close the lid, and secure to the locking position. Be sure the vent is turned to sealing. Set for 25 minutes on Manual at high pressure.

6. Let the pressure release naturally.

7. Carefully remove the cake pan with the handles of the steaming rack and allow to stand for 10 minutes before cutting and serving.

Kelly's Company Omelette

Kelly Bailey, Dillsburg, PA

Makes 12 servings
Prep. Time: 15 minutes & Cooking Time: 7–9 hours & Ideal slow-cooker size: 6-qt.

32-oz. bag frozen hash brown potatoes, or 5 cups cooked, shredded potatoes

1 lb. ham, bacon, or sausage, cooked and chopped

1 onion, chopped

1 green bell pepper, chopped

1 cup sliced fresh mushrooms

2 cups shredded cheddar cheese

12 eggs

1 cup whole milk

1 Tbsp. thyme, basil, rosemary, or tarragon, depending on what you like

½ tsp. cayenne pepper

1. In lightly greased slow cooker, place ⅓ of potatoes, ⅓ of ham, ⅓ of onion, ⅓ of green pepper, ⅓ of mushrooms, and ⅓ of cheese.

2. Repeat layers twice, ending with cheese.

3. In mixing bowl, whisk together eggs, milk, the herb you chose, and cayenne.

4. Pour gently over the layers in the slow cooker.

5. Cover and cook on Low 7–9 hours, until omelette is set in the middle and lightly browned at edges.

Breakfast for Dinner   19

Southwestern Egg Casserole

Eileen Eash, Lafayette, CO

Makes 12 servings
Prep. Time: 10 minutes ❧ Cooking Time: 20 minutes

1 cup water
2½ cups egg substitute
½ cup flour
1 tsp. baking powder
⅛ tsp. salt
⅛ tsp. pepper
2 cups cottage cheese
1½ cups shredded sharp cheddar cheese
¼ cup margarine, melted
2 (4-oz.) cans chopped green chilies

1. Place the steaming rack into the bottom of the inner pot and pour in 1 cup of water.

2. Grease a round 7-inch springform pan.

3. Combine the egg substitute, flour, baking powder, salt, and pepper in a mixing bowl. It will be lumpy.

4. Stir in the cheeses, margarine, and green chilies then pour into the springform pan.

5. Place the springform pan onto the steaming rack, close the lid, and secure to the locking position. Be sure the vent is turned to sealing. Manually set the cook time for 20 minutes on high pressure.

6. When cook time is up, let the pressure release naturally.

7. Carefully remove the springform pan with the handles of the steaming rack and allow to stand 10 minutes before cutting and serving.

Breakfast for Dinner Casserole

Hope Comerford, Clinton Township, MI

Makes 4–6 servings
Prep. Time: 15 minutes · Cooking Time: 25 minutes

1 Tbsp. olive oil
½ lb. bulk breakfast sausage
½ cup finely diced onion
1 cup water
½ lb. frozen Tater Tots or hash browns
6 eggs
¼ cup half-and-half
½ tsp. salt
½ tsp. garlic powder
¼ tsp. black pepper
⅛ tsp. cayenne pepper
½ cup diced bell pepper (any color you wish)
1 cup shredded pepper Jack cheese
½ cup shredded cheddar cheese

1. Set the Instant Pot to the Sauté function and add the olive oil.

2. Add the bulk sausage and onion to the inner pot of the Instant Pot and cook until browned. Remove it from the Instant Pot and set aside. Press the Cancel button.

3. Carefully wipe out the inside of the Instant Pot. Pour in the water and scrape the bottom, to be sure there is nothing stuck. Place the trivet on top with handles up.

4. Grease a 7-inch baking pan with butter or nonstick cooking spray. Arrange the Tater Tots or hash browns evenly around the bottom of the pan.

5. In a bowl, mix the eggs, half-and-half, salt, garlic powder, black pepper, and cayenne. Stir in the bell pepper and pepper Jack cheese. Pour this over the hash browns.

6. Sprinkle the cheddar over the top of the casserole. Cover with foil. Carefully lower the baking pan onto the trivet.

7. Secure the lid and set the vent to sealing. Manually set the cook time for 25 minutes on high pressure.

8. When the cook time is over, let the pressure release naturally for 10 minutes, then manually release the remaining pressure.

9. With hot pads, carefully remove the baking pan with the handles of the trivet. Uncover, serve, and enjoy!

Variations:

You can use any types of cheese that your family likes. You do not have to stick with what is suggested above. Also, you could use bacon instead of sausage, or omit the meat altogether.

Breakfast Burrito Casserole

Hope Comerford, Clinton Township, MI

Makes 6 burritos
*Prep. Time: 5–7 minutes * *Cooking Time: 13 minutes*

1 tsp. olive oil
8 oz. ground chorizo
⅓ cup chopped onion
1 poblano pepper, seeded and diced
16 oz. frozen diced potatoes
1 cup + 1 Tbsp. water, *divided*
4 eggs
¼ tsp. salt
¼ tsp. pepper
⅓ cup shredded Mexican blend cheese (or any cheese of your liking)
¼ cup of your favorite salsa, *optional*
6 flour tortillas

1. Set the Instant Pot to the Sauté function and heat the olive oil.

2. Add in the chorizo, onion, and poblano pepper, and sauté until browned, about 5 minutes.

3. Add in the potatoes and sauté for about 5 minutes longer.

4. Remove the chorizo/potato mix from the inner pot and set aside.

5. Pour 1 cup of water into the inner pot and scrape up any bits on the bottom of the pot.

6. Place the trivet with handles into the inner pot.

7. In a bowl, mix the eggs, tablespoon of water, salt, and pepper. Stir in the chorizo/potato mix.

8. Spray a 7-inch round baking pan with nonstick spray. Pour the egg/chorizo/potato mix into the pan and sprinkle with the cheese. Cover with foil.

9. Place the pan on top of the trivet. Secure the lid and set the vent to sealing.

10. Manually set the cook time for 13 minutes on high pressure.

11. When cook time is up, let the pressure release naturally.

12. When the pin drops, remove the lid and then carefully remove the baking pan from the trivet.

13. Fill the tortillas with some of the filling, add salsa if desired, and wrap up like a burrito.

24   Fix-It and Forget-It Simple & Satisfying

Overnight Mexican Breakfast Casserole

Carrie Fritz, Meridian, ID

Makes 6–8 servings
Prep. Time: 20 minutes ❖ Cooking Time: 6–8 hours ❖ Ideal slow-cooker size: 6-qt.

30-oz. bag frozen shredded hash brown potatoes
1 lb. spicy sausage, cooked and crumbled
2 cups shredded sharp or cheddar cheese
1 green or red bell pepper, chopped
¾ cup sliced green onion
4-oz. can chopped green chiles
12 eggs
1 cup milk
½ tsp. salt
¼ tsp. pepper

1. Grease slow cooker.

2. Layer in half the hash browns, half the sausage, half the cheese, half the green onions, half the peppers, and half the chiles.

3. Repeat layers.

4. In a mixing bowl, whisk eggs, milk, salt, and pepper.

5. Pour egg mixture gently over layers in slow cooker.

6. Cover and cook on Low for 6–8 hours.

Variation:
Cooked ham or bacon works in place of the sausage.

Tip:
Add ½ tsp. chili powder and ½ tsp. dried oregano. Use Mexican blend cheese in place of cheddar.

Fiesta Hashbrowns

Dena Mell-Dorchy, Royal Oak, MI

Makes 8 servings
Prep. Time: 15 minutes   Cooking Time: 8–9 hours   Ideal slow-cooker size: 3- or 4-qt.

1 lb. ground turkey sausage
½ cup chopped onion
5 cups gluten-free frozen diced hash browns
8 oz. gluten-free low-sodium chicken stock
1 small red sweet pepper
1 jalapeño, seeded and finely diced
1½ cups sliced mushrooms
2 Tbsp. quick-cooking tapioca
½ cup shredded Monterey Jack cheese

1. Spray slow cooker with nonstick spray.

2. In a large skillet, brown sausage and onion over medium heat. Drain off fat.

3. Combine sausage mixture, hash browns, chicken stock, sweet pepper, jalapeño, mushrooms, and quick-cooking tapioca in cooker; stir to combine.

4. Cover and cook on Low for 8–9 hours. Stir before serving. Top with shredded Monterey Jack cheese.

Breakfast for Dinner

Potato-Bacon Gratin

Valerie Drobel, Carlisle, PA

Makes 8 (5-oz.) servings
Prep. Time: 20 minutes   ❦   Cooking Time: 40 minutes

1 Tbsp. olive oil

6-oz. bag fresh spinach

1 clove garlic, minced

4 large potatoes, peeled or unpeeled, *divided*

6 oz. Canadian bacon slices, *divided*

5 oz. grated Swiss cheddar, *divided*

1 cup chicken broth

1. Set the Instant Pot to Sauté and pour in the olive oil. Cook the spinach and garlic in olive oil just until spinach is wilted (5 minutes or less). Press Cancel.

2. Cut potatoes into thin slices, about ¼-inch thick.

3. Spray a 7-inch springform pan with nonstick spray, then layer ⅓ the potatoes, half the bacon, ⅓ the cheese, and half the wilted spinach.

4. Repeat layers ending with potatoes. Reserve ⅓ cheese for later.

5. Pour chicken broth over contents of pot.

6. Wipe the bottom of the inner pot to soak up any remaining oil, then add in 2 cups of water and the steaming rack. Place the springform pan on top.

7. Close the lid and secure to the locking position. Be sure the vent is turned to sealing. Manually set the cook time for 35 minutes on high pressure.

8. When cook time is up, manually release the pressure.

9. Top with the remaining cheese, then allow to stand 10 minutes before removing from the Instant Pot, cutting, and serving.

Breakfast for Dinner

Italian Sausage and Sweet Pepper Hash

Hope Comerford, Clinton Township, MI

Makes 6–8 servings
Prep. Time: 10 minutes ❧ Cooking Time: 6½ hours ❧ Ideal slow-cooker size: 4-qt.

12-oz. pkg. Italian turkey sausage, cut lengthwise, then into ½-inch pieces
16 oz. frozen diced potatoes
1½ cups sliced sweet onion
1 yellow pepper, sliced
1 green pepper, sliced
1 red pepper, sliced
¼ cup melted butter
1 tsp. sea salt
½ tsp. pepper
½ tsp. dried thyme
½ tsp. dried parsley
½ cup shredded reduced-fat Swiss cheese

1. Spray crock with nonstick spray.

2. Place sausage, frozen potatoes, onion, and sliced peppers into crock.

3. Mix melted butter with salt, pepper, thyme, and parsley. Pour over contents of crock and stir.

4. Cover and cook on Low for 6 hours. Sprinkle with the Swiss cheese, then cover and cook for an additional 20 minutes, or until the cheese is melted.

Overnight French Toast

Rebekah Zehr, Lowville, NY

Makes 8 servings
Prep. Time: 20 minutes ❧ Cooking Time: 7 hours ❧ Ideal slow-cooker size: 5-qt.

- 1 cup brown sugar
- 8 Tbsp. (1 stick) butter, room temperature
- 2 Tbsp. corn syrup
- 16-oz. loaf multigrain French bread in 1-inch slices
- 4 eggs
- 1 cup milk
- 1 tsp. vanilla extract
- ¼ cup orange juice
- ¼ tsp. ground cinnamon
- ⅛ tsp. ground allspice

1. Turn slow cooker on High.

2. Place brown sugar, butter, and corn syrup in crock. Heat until melted, about 1 hour. Stir to combine.

3. Lay bread slices on the top of the syrup mixture, fitting tightly together.

4. Whisk together remaining ingredients and pour over top of bread.

5. Cover and cook on Low for 6 hours.

6. Remove crock from cooker and invert French toast onto serving platter.

Variations:

After cooking syrup, mix in pecans in Step 2 and continue with directions. May melt syrup ingredients in microwave or saucepan if you don't want to wait for the slow cooker to melt them.

Breakfast for Dinner

Cinnamon French Toast Casserole

Hope Comerford, Clinton Township, MI

Makes 8 servings
Prep. Time: 10 minutes   &   Cooking Time: 20 minutes

3 eggs

2 cups milk

¼ cup maple syrup

1 tsp. vanilla extract

1 tsp. cinnamon

Pinch salt

16-oz. loaf cinnamon swirl bread, cubed and left out overnight to go stale

1 cup water

Serving suggestion:

Serve with whipped cream and fresh fruit on top, with an extra sprinkle of cinnamon.

1. In a medium bowl, whisk together the eggs, milk, maple syrup, vanilla, cinnamon, and salt. Stir in the cubes of cinnamon swirl bread.

2. You will need a 7-inch round pan for this. Spray the inside with nonstick cooking spray, then pour the bread mixture into the pan.

3. Place the trivet in the bottom of the inner pot, then pour in the water.

4. Make a foil sling and insert it onto the trivet. Carefully place the 7-inch pan on top of the foil sling/trivet.

5. Secure the lid to the locked position, then make sure the vent is turned to sealing.

6. Press the Manual button and use the "+/-" button to set the Instant Pot for 20 minutes.

7. When the cook time is over, let the Instant Pot release naturally for 5 minutes, then quick release the rest.

Overnight Steel-Cut Oatmeal

Lavina Hochstedler, Grand Blanc, MI

Makes 10 servings
Prep. Time: 5 minutes ❧ Cooking Time: 6–8 hours ❧ Ideal slow-cooker size: 3-qt.

1 cup steel-cut oats, uncooked
1 cup dried cranberries
1 cup dried, chopped apricots
3 cups water
1½ cups milk
Pinch salt, *optional*

1. Combine all ingredients in slow cooker.
2. Cover and cook on Low for 6–8 hours. Stir again. Serve hot.

Tips:

Mix this up before bed and have it hot for breakfast in the morning. If you have a newer slow cooker, it may cook hot, so reduce the time and use a timer or the programmable feature on the cooker. Do not use instant steel-cut oats!

Serving suggestions:

- Top with vanilla or plain yogurt.
- Great with a half grapefruit and a cup of coffee.

Overnight Oat Groats

Rebekah Zehr, Lowville, NY

Makes 6 servings
Prep. Time: 5 minutes ❧ Cooking Time: 8–10 hours ❧ Ideal slow-cooker size: 3-qt.

1½ cups oat groats
4 cups water
2 cups almond milk or milk
1–2 cinnamon sticks
½ cup brown sugar
½–1 cup dried apples
2 scoops vanilla-flavored protein powder, *optional*

1. Combine all ingredients in slow cooker.
2. Cook on Low for 8–10 hours.

Serving suggestion:

Serve with a variety of toppings including coconut, nuts, granola, chia seeds, and yogurt.

Breakfast for Dinner

German Chocolate Oatmeal

Hope Comerford, Clinton Township, MI

Makes 4 servings
Prep. Time: 5 minutes ❖ Cooking Time: 6–8 hours ❖ Ideal slow-cooker size: 3-qt.

2 cups steel-cut oats
8 cups unsweetened coconut milk
¼ cup unsweetened cocoa powder
¼ tsp. kosher salt
Sweetened shredded coconut, to taste

1. Spray crock with nonstick spray.

2. Place steel-cut oats, coconut milk, cocoa powder, and salt into crock and stir to mix.

3. Cover and cook on Low for 6–8 hours.

4. To serve, top each bowl of oatmeal with desired amount of shredded coconut.

Serving suggestion:

When serving, sweeten with a bit of sweetener of your choice if you wish.

Breakfast for Dinner 37

Apple Cinnamon Oatmeal

Hope Comerford, Clinton Township, MI

Makes 2–3 servings

Prep. Time: 5 minutes & Cooking Time: 7 hours & Ideal slow-cooker size: 2-qt.

½ cup steel-cut oats
2 cups unsweetened nondairy milk
1 small apple, peeled and diced
½ tsp. vanilla extract
¼ tsp. cinnamon

1. Spray crock with nonstick spray.
2. Place all ingredients into crock and stir lightly.
3. Cover and cook on Low for 7 hours.

Serving suggestion:

Add a bit of honey if you wish at time of serving.

Soups, Stews, Chilis & Chowders

Chicken

Chicken Noodle Soup

Colleen Heatwole, Burton, MI

Makes 6–8 servings
Prep. Time: 15 minutes Cooking Time: 4 minutes

2 Tbsp. butter
1 Tbsp. oil
1 medium onion, diced
2 large carrots, diced
3 celery stalks, diced
Salt to taste
3 cloves garlic, minced
1 tsp. thyme
1 tsp. oregano
1 tsp. basil
8 cups chicken broth
2 cups cubed cooked chicken
8 oz. medium egg noodles
1 cup peas (if frozen, thaw while preparing soup)
Pepper to taste

1. In the inner pot of the Instant Pot, melt the butter with oil on the Sauté function.

2. Add the onion, carrots, and celery with a large pinch of salt and continue cooking on Sauté until soft, about 5 minutes, stirring frequently.

3. Add the garlic, thyme, oregano, and basil and sauté an additional minute.

4. Add the broth, cooked chicken, and noodles, stirring to combine all ingredients.

5. Put the lid on the Instant Pot and set the vent to sealing. Manually set the cook time for 4 minutes on high pressure.

6. When time is up, manually release the pressure.

7. When the pin drops, remove the lid and add the thawed peas, stir, adjust seasoning with salt and pepper, and serve.

Soups, Stews, Chilis & Chowders: Chicken

Chicken and Corn Soup

Eleanor Larson, Glen Lyon, PA

Makes 4–6 servings
Prep. Time: 15 minutes　※　Cooking Time: 8–9 hours　※　Ideal slow-cooker size: 4-qt.

2 whole boneless, skinless chicken breasts, cubed
1 onion, chopped
1 garlic clove, minced
2 carrots, sliced
2 ribs celery, chopped
2 medium potatoes, cubed
1 tsp. mixed dried herbs
⅓ cup tomato sauce
12-oz. can cream-style corn
14-oz. can whole kernel corn
3 cups chicken stock
¼ cup chopped Italian parsley
1 tsp. salt
¼ tsp. pepper

1. Combine all ingredients except parsley, salt, and pepper in slow cooker.

2. Cover. Cook on Low 8–9 hours, or until chicken is tender.

3. Add parsley and seasonings 30 minutes before serving.

Fix-It and Forget-It Simple & Satisfying

Easy Chicken Tortilla Soup

Becky Harder, Monument, CO

Makes 6–8 servings
Prep. Time: 5–10 minutes ❧ Cooking Time: 8 hours ❧ Ideal slow-cooker size: 4- to 5-qt.

4 chicken breast halves

2 (15-oz.) cans black beans, undrained

2 (15-oz.) cans Mexican stewed tomatoes, or Ro*Tel tomatoes

1 cup salsa (mild, medium, or hot, whichever you prefer)

4-oz. can chopped green chilies

14½-oz. can tomato sauce

Tortilla chips

Shredded cheese

1. Combine all ingredients in large slow cooker.

2. Cover. Cook on Low 8 hours.

3. Just before serving, remove chicken breasts and slice into bite-sized pieces. Stir into soup.

4. Put a handful of tortilla chips in each individual soup bowl. Ladle soup over chips. Top with shredded cheese.

Soups, Stews, Chilis & Chowders: Chicken   45

Black Bean Soup with Chicken and Salsa

Hope Comerford, Clinton Township, MI

Makes 4–6 servings
Prep. Time: 10 minutes ❧ Cooking Time: 6–8 hours ❧ Ideal slow-cooker size: 5- to 6-qt.

4 cups chicken broth
1 large boneless, skinless chicken breast
2 (15-oz.) cans black beans, rinsed and drained
16-oz. jar salsa
1 cup frozen corn
1 cup sliced fresh mushrooms
½ red onion, chopped
1 jalapeño (whole)
1½ tsp. cumin
Salt and pepper to taste

Optional Toppings:
Shredded cheese
Sour cream
Cilantro
Avocado

1. Place all ingredients except the toppings in slow cooker. Stir.

2. Cover and cook on Low for 6–8 hours.

3. Remove the chicken and shred between two forks. Replace back in the soup and stir.

4. Serve garnished with the optional toppings.

Variation:

You may chop up the jalapeño for extra heat. Leaving it whole provides the flavor without the heat.

46 Fix-It and Forget-It Simple & Satisfying

Chicken Stew

Hope Comerford, Clinton Township, MI

Makes 6 servings
Prep. Time: 10 minutes & Cooking Time: 20 minutes

1 Tbsp. olive oil
1 cup chopped onion
3 carrots, chopped
2 celery stalks, chopped
4 cups chicken broth, *divided*
2 lb. boneless, skinless chicken breasts, diced
4–5 red potatoes, chopped
2½ tsp. salt
3 tsp. garlic powder
3 tsp. onion powder
1½ tsp. Italian seasoning
¼ tsp. pepper
2 bay leaves
2 Tbsp. cornstarch
2 Tbsp. cold water

1. Press Sauté on the Instant Pot. Let it get hot. Add the oil.

2. Sauté the onion, carrots, and celery for about 3–5 minutes.

3. Pour in 1 cup of the broth and scrape the bottom of the inner pot to bring up any stuck-on bits. Press Cancel.

4. Add the chicken, red potatoes, salt, garlic powder, onion powder, Italian seasoning, pepper, bay leaves, and remaining 3 cups of broth.

5. Secure the lid and set the vent to sealing. Manually set the cook time for 10 minutes on high pressure.

6. When cook time is up, let the pressure release naturally for 10 minutes, then manually release the remaining pressure. When the pin drops, remove the lid. Press Cancel.

7. Press the Sauté function once again. Mix the cornstarch and cold water, then stir it into the stew. Let it simmer for about 5 minutes, or until it is thickened. Remove the bay leaves before serving.

Serving suggestion:

Serve with buttered crusty Italian or French bread.

White Chicken Chili

Lucille Hollinger, Richland, PA

Makes 8 servings
Prep. Time: 10 minutes ❧ Cooking Time: 5–6 hours ❧ Ideal slow-cooker size: 3-qt.

4 cups cubed cooked chicken
2 cups chicken broth
2 (14½-oz.) cans cannellini beans
14½-oz. can garbanzo beans
1 cup shredded white cheddar cheese
¼ cup chopped onion
¼ cup chopped bell pepper
2 tsp. ground cumin
½ tsp. dried oregano
¼ tsp. cayenne pepper
¼ tsp. salt

1. Combine all ingredients in slow cooker.
2. Cover and cook on Low for 5–6 hours.

Variations:

Omit garbanzo beans. Shred chicken instead of cubing it. Add 1 tsp. Italian herb seasoning.

—Beverly Hummel

Serving suggestion:
Serve with cornbread and salad.

Soups, Stews, Chilis & Chowders: Chicken ❧ 49

Pork

Italian Shredded Pork Stew

Emily Fox, Bernville, PA

Makes: 6–8 servings
Prep. Time: 20 minutes ❧ Cooking Time: 8–10 hours ❧ Ideal slow-cooker size: 5-qt.

2 medium sweet potatoes, peeled and cubed
2 cups chopped fresh kale
1 large onion, chopped
3 cloves garlic, minced
2½–3½-lb. boneless pork shoulder butt roast
14-oz. can white kidney or cannellini beans, drained
1½ tsp. Italian seasoning
½ tsp. salt
½ tsp. pepper
3 (14½-oz.) cans chicken broth
Sour cream, *optional*

1. Place first four ingredients in slow cooker.
2. Place roast on vegetables.
3. Add beans and seasonings.
4. Pour the broth over top.
5. Cover and cook on Low 8–10 hours or until meat is tender.
6. Remove meat. Skim fat from cooking juices if desired. Shred pork with two forks and return to cooker. Heat through.
7. Garnish with sour cream if desired.

Soups, Stews, Chilis & Chowders: Pork

The Best Bean and Ham Soup

Hope Comerford, Clinton Township, MI

Makes 8–10 servings
Prep. Time: 10 minutes ❦ Soaking Time: 12–24 hours ❦ Cooking Time: 40 minutes

1 Tbsp. olive oil
1 cup chopped onion
2 cloves garlic, minced
1 cup chopped celery
8–10 cups water, *divided*
1 meaty ham bone or shank
1 lb. dry navy beans, soaked overnight, rinsed and drained
¼ cup chopped parsley
1 Tbsp. salt
1 tsp. pepper
1 tsp. nutmeg
1 tsp. oregano
1 tsp. basil
1 bay leaf
1 cup mashed potato flakes

1. Set the Instant Pot to Sauté and add in the olive oil to heat.

2. Sauté the onions, garlic, and celery for 5 minutes.

3. Pour in 1 cup of water and scrape any bits off the bottom of the Inner Pot. Press Cancel.

4. Place the ham bone in inner pot, then pour in all the remaining ingredients except water and mashed potato flakes.

5. Fill with the remaining water, or until ⅔ of the way full.

6. Secure the lid and set the vent to sealing. Manually set the cook time for 35 minutes on high pressure.

7. When cook time is up, let the pressure release naturally.

8. When the pin drops, carefully remove the lid and stir in the mashed potato flakes. Remove bay leaf. Let the soup thicken for a few minutes, then serve.

Ham and Bean Stew

Sharon Wantland, Menomonee Falls, WI

Makes 4–6 servings
Prep. Time: 15 minutes ❧ Cooking Time: 5–7 hours ❧ Ideal slow-cooker size: 3-qt.

2 (16-oz.) cans baked beans
2 medium potatoes, peeled and cubed
2 cups cubed ham
2 ribs celery, chopped
1 onion, chopped
½ cup water
1 Tbsp. cider vinegar
1 tsp. salt
⅛ tsp. pepper

1. In a slow cooker combine all ingredients. Mix well.

2. Cover and cook on Low for 5–7 hours, or until the potatoes are tender.

Soups, Stews, Chilis & Chowders: Pork

Kielbasa Soup

Hope Comerford, Clinton Township, MI

Makes 8 servings
Prep. Time: 10 minutes & Cooking Time: 10 hours & Ideal slow-cooker size: 8-qt.

6-oz. can tomato paste
1 medium onion, chopped
3 medium potatoes, diced
2 cups chopped cabbage
½ cup chopped carrot
½ cup chopped celery
½ cup frozen green chopped green beans
2 lb. kielbasa, cut into ¼-inch pieces
2 tsp. salt
1 tsp. oregano
1 tsp. thyme
½ tsp. pepper
6 cups water
6 cups chicken stock

1. Combine all ingredients in crock.
2. Cover. Cook on Low 10 hours.

Split Pea Soup

Kelly Amos, Pittsboro, NC

Makes 8 servings
Prep. Time: 10 minutes ❧ Cooking Time: 8–9 hours ❧ Ideal slow-cooker size: 4½-qt.

2 cups dry split peas
8 cups water
2 onions, chopped
2 carrots, peeled and sliced
4 slices Canadian bacon, chopped
2 Tbsp. chicken bouillon granules, or 2 chicken bouillon cubes
1 tsp. salt
¼–½ tsp. pepper

1. Combine all ingredients in slow cooker.
2. Cover. Cook on Low 8–9 hours.

Variation:

For a creamier soup, remove half of soup when done and puree. Stir back into rest of soup.

Potato Soup

Michele Ruvola, Vestal, NY

Makes 4 servings
Prep. Time: 20 minutes   Cooking Time: 5 minutes

5 lb. russet potatoes, peeled and cubed
3 celery stalks, sliced thin
1 large onion, diced
1 clove garlic, minced
1 Tbsp. seasoning salt
1 tsp. ground black pepper
¼ cup butter
1 lb. bacon, fried crisp, rough chopped
4 cups chicken stock
1 cup heavy cream
½ cup whole milk

Optional Garnishes:
Sour cream
Shredded cheddar cheese
Sliced green onions

1. Put potatoes, celery, onion, garlic, seasoning salt, pepper, and butter in the inner pot of the Instant Pot. Stir to combine.

2. Add bacon and chicken stock, then stir to combine.

3. Secure the lid and make sure the vent is on sealing. Push the Manual mode button, then set timer for 5 minutes on high pressure.

4. Quick release the steam when cook time is up.

5. Remove lid; mash potatoes to make a semismooth soup.

6. Add cream and milk; stir to combine.

7. Serve with garnishes if desired.

Serving suggestion:
Perfect on a cold night with slices of bread on the side or a salad.

Soups, Stews, Chilis & Chowders: Pork

Creamy Potato Chowder

Emily Fox, Bernville, PA

Makes 8 servings
Prep. Time: 15 minutes ❖ Cooking Time: 8–10 hours ❖ Ideal slow-cooker size: 5-qt.

8 cups diced potatoes
5½ cups chicken broth
10½-oz. can cream of chicken soup
⅓ cup chopped onion
¼ tsp. pepper
8 oz. cream cheese, cubed
½ lb. bacon, cooked
Crumbled minced chives

1. Combine the first five ingredients in the crock.

2. Cover and cook on Low 8–10 hours.

3. Add cream cheese; stir until blended. Garnish with bacon and chives.

Beef

Beef Vegetable Soup

Anona M. Teel, Bangor, PA

Makes 6 servings
Prep. Time: 15 minutes & Cooking Time: 8–10 hours & Ideal slow-cooker size: 6½-qt.

1–1½-lb. soup bone
1 lb. stewing beef cubes
1½ qt. cold water
1 Tbsp. salt
¾ cup diced celery
¾ cup diced carrots
¾ cup diced potatoes
¾ cup diced onion
1 cup frozen mixed vegetables of your choice
16-oz. can diced tomatoes
⅛ tsp. pepper
1 Tbsp. chopped dried parsley

1. Put all ingredients in slow cooker.

2. Cover. Cook on Low 8–10 hours. Remove bone before serving.

Soups, Stews, Chilis & Chowders: Beef

Beef Mushroom Barley Soup

Becky Frey, Lebanon, PA

Makes 8 servings
Prep. Time: 20 minutes • Cooking Time: 25 minutes

- 2 Tbsp. olive oil, *divided*
- 1 lb. boneless beef chuck, cubed
- 1 large onion, chopped
- 2 cloves garlic, crushed
- 1 lb. fresh mushrooms, sliced
- 1 celery stalk, sliced
- 2 carrots, sliced
- ½ tsp. dried thyme, *optional*
- 8 cups low-sodium beef stock
- ½ cup uncooked pearl barley
- ½ tsp. freshly ground pepper
- 3 Tbsp. chopped fresh parsley

1. Set the Instant Pot to the Sauté function and heat up 1 Tbsp. of the olive oil in the inner pot.

2. Brown the beef, in batches if needed, and then remove and set aside.

3. Add the remaining Tbsp. of olive oil and sauté the onion, garlic, and mushrooms for 3–4 minutes.

4. Add the beef back in, as well as all the remaining ingredients, except for the parsley. Press Cancel.

5. Secure the lid and set the vent to sealing.

6. Manually set the cook time to 25 minutes on high pressure.

7. When the cooking time is over, let the pressure release naturally for 15 minutes, then manually release the remaining pressure.

8. When the pin drops, remove the lid, and stir. Serve each bowl topped with some fresh chopped parsley.

Beef Stew

Carol Eveleth, Hillsdale, WY

Makes 10 servings
Prep. Time: 20 minutes ❧ Cooking Time: 5–7 hours ❧ Ideal slow-cooker size: 5-qt.

2-lb. boneless beef chuck roast, cut into 1-inch chunks
6 large carrots, sliced, chopped
4 medium potatoes, peeled or not, chopped
4 ribs celery, sliced, chopped
1 large onion, chopped
3 tsp. salt
¼ tsp. black pepper
3 Tbsp. quick-cooking tapioca
½ cup ketchup
1 cup tomato juice
1 cup water

1. Grease interior of slow-cooker crock.

2. Place beef, carrots, potatoes, celery, and onion in crock.

3. Sprinkle seasonings and tapioca on top.

4. Pour ketchup, tomato juice, and water over contents of crock. Stir everything together well.

5. Cover. Cook for 5–7 hours on Low, or until instant-read meat thermometer registers 145°F when stuck in center of beef chunks and vegetables are as tender as you like them.

68   **Fix-It and Forget-It Simple & Satisfying**

Tuscan Beef Stew

Orpha Herr, Andover, NY

Makes 12 servings

Prep. Time: 20 minutes & Cooking Time: 8½–9½ hours & Ideal slow-cooker size: 6-qt.

Ingredients:
- 10¾-oz. can tomato soup
- 1½ cups beef broth
- ½ cup burgundy wine or other red wine
- 1 tsp. Italian herb seasoning
- ½ tsp. garlic powder
- 14½-oz. can diced Italian-style tomatoes, undrained
- ½ cup diced onion
- 3 large carrots, cut in 1-inch pieces
- 2 lb. stew beef, cut into 1-inch pieces
- 2 (16-oz.) cans cannellini beans, rinsed and drained

1. Stir soup, broth, wine, Italian seasoning, garlic powder, tomatoes, onion, carrots, and beef into slow cooker.

2. Cover and cook on Low 8–9 hours or until vegetables are tender-crisp.

3. Stir in beans. Turn to High until heated through, 10–20 minutes more.

Chili Comerford-Style

Hope Comerford, Clinton Township, MI

Makes 4–6 servings
Prep. Time: 10 minutes Cooking Time: 15 minutes

1 tsp. olive oil

1 lb. ground round

1 medium onion, chopped

15½-oz. can kidney beans, rinsed and drained

2 (14½-oz.) cans diced tomatoes

10-oz. can cream of tomato soup (I use Pacific Foods Creamy Tomato)

3 cloves garlic, minced

2 tsp. tarragon

1 tsp. salt

1 tsp. pepper

2 tsp. chili powder

1 cup beef stock

3–6 cups water, depending on how thick or thin you like your chili

1. Set the Instant Pot to the Sauté function and let it get hot. Pour in the olive oil and coat the bottom of the pot.

2. Brown the ground round with the onion. This will take about 5–7 minutes.

3. Press Cancel. Carefully drain the grease.

4. Place the remaining ingredients into the inner pot with the beef and onion.

5. Secure the lid and set the vent to sealing. Manually set the cook time for 15 minutes on high pressure.

6. When cook time is up, manually release the pressure. When the pin drops, remove the lid and serve.

Serving suggestion:

We love to add a dollop of sour cream and a bit of shredded sharp cheddar to our chili.

Soups, Stews, Chilis & Chowders: Beef

Chipotle Beef Chili

Karen Ceneviva, Seymour, CT

Makes 8 servings
Prep. Time: 10–15 minutes ❧ Cooking Time: 4–9 hours ❧ Ideal slow-cooker size: 3½-qt.

16-oz. jar chunky chipotle salsa
1 cup water
2 tsp. chili powder
1 tsp. salt
1 large onion, chopped
2 lb. stewing beef, cut into ½-inch pieces
19-oz. can red kidney beans, rinsed and drained

1. Stir all ingredients together in slow cooker.

2. Cover. Cook on High 4–5 hours or on Low 8–9 hours, until beef is fork-tender.

Meatless

Veggie Minestrone

Dorothy VanDeest, Memphis, TN

Makes 8 servings
Prep. Time: 5 minutes   Cooking Time: 4 minutes

2 Tbsp. olive oil

1 large onion, chopped

1 garlic clove, minced

4 cups low-sodium chicken stock or vegetable stock

16-oz. can kidney beans, rinsed and drained

14½-oz. can no-salt-added diced tomatoes

2 medium carrots, sliced thin

¼ tsp. dried oregano

¼ tsp. pepper

½ cup whole wheat elbow macaroni, uncooked

4 oz. fresh spinach

½ cup grated Parmesan cheese

1. Set the Instant Pot to the Sauté function and heat the olive oil.

2. When the olive oil is heated, add the onion and garlic to the inner pot and sauté for 5 minutes.

3. Press Cancel and add the stock, kidney beans, tomatoes, carrots, oregano, and pepper. Gently pour in the macaroni, but *do not stir*. Just push the noodles gently under the liquid.

4. Secure the lid and set the vent to sealing.

5. Manually set the cook time for 4 minutes on high pressure.

6. When the cooking time is over, manually release the pressure and remove the lid when the pin drops.

7. Stir in the spinach and let wilt a few minutes.

8. Sprinkle 1 Tbsp. grated Parmesan on each individual bowl of this soup. Enjoy!

Soups, Stews, Chilis & Chowders: Meatless

Super Healthy Cabbage Soup

Hope Comerford, Clinton Township, MI

Makes 8–10 servings
Prep. Time: 10 minutes • Cooking Time: 5 minutes

1 Tbsp. olive oil
1½ cups chopped onion
3 carrots, halved and sliced
2 celery stalks, halved and sliced
3–4 cups vegetable broth or chicken broth, *divided*
14½-oz. can diced tomatoes
3 cups chopped cabbage
1 jalapeño, seeded and diced
1 Tbsp. garlic powder
3 tsp. salt
1 tsp. basil
1 tsp. oregano
¼ tsp. pepper
46 oz. no-salt-added tomato juice

1. Turn the Instant Pot to the Sauté function and let it get hot. Add the olive oil.

2. Sauté the onions, carrots, and celery for 3–5 minutes. Add 1 cup of the broth and scrape the bottom of the inner pot to get off any stuck-on bits. Press Cancel.

3. Add the remaining ingredients, including the remaining broth. You do not want to fill your pot all the way to the fill line. So, use a bit less broth if needed to not reach fill line.

4. Secure the lid and set the vent to sealing. Manually set the cook time for 5 minutes on high pressure.

5. When cook time is up, let the pressure release naturally for 10 minutes, then manually release the remaining pressure.

Mediterranean Lentil Soup

Marcia S. Myer, Manheim, PA

Makes 6 servings
Prep. Time: 10 minutes & Cooking Time: 18 minutes

2 Tbsp. olive oil
2 large onions, chopped
1 carrot, chopped
1 cup uncooked lentils
½ tsp. dried thyme
½ tsp. dried marjoram
3 cups low-sodium chicken stock or vegetable stock
14½-oz. can diced no-salt-added tomatoes
¼ cup chopped fresh parsley
¼ cup sherry, *optional*
⅔ cup grated low-fat cheese, *optional*

1. Set the Instant Pot to the Sauté function, then heat up the olive oil.

2. Sauté the onions and carrot until the onions are translucent, about 5 minutes.

3. Press the Cancel button, then add the lentils, thyme, marjoram, stock, and canned tomatoes.

4. Secure the lid and set the vent to sealing.

5. Manually set the cook time to 18 minutes at high pressure.

6. When the cooking time is over, manually release the pressure.

7. When the pin drops, stir in the parsley and sherry (if using).

8. When serving, add a sprinkle of grated low-fat cheese if you wish.

Slow-Cooker Adaptation:

1. Add all ingredients, except the parsley, sherry, and cheese, to a 5- to 6-qt. slow-cooker crock.

2. Cover and cook on Low for 7 hours, or on High for 3½ hours.

3. When cook time is up, stir in the parsley and sherry (if using).

4. When serving, add a sprinkle of grated low-fat cheese if you wish.

Soups, Stews, Chilis & Chowders: Meatless

Spicy Black Bean Sweet Potato Stew

Maria Shevlin, Sicklerville, NJ

Makes 3–4 servings
Prep. Time: 5 minutes ❧ Cooking Time: 10 minutes

2 tsp. olive oil

4 cloves garlic, minced

1 large onion, diced

8-oz. pkg. mushrooms, chopped

1¾ cups water

2 (14½-oz.) cans petite diced tomatoes

15½-oz. can black beans, rinsed and drained

4 sweet potatoes, peeled and cubed

1 vegetable bouillon cube

1 Tbsp. garlic powder

1 Tbsp. onion powder

1 Tbsp. parsley flakes

2 tsp. paprika

1 tsp. cumin

3 heaping Tbsp. creole seasoning, *optional*

1. Set the Instant Pot to Sauté, then add the olive oil, garlic, and onion. Cook until just translucent.

2. Add the mushrooms and cook for 2 minutes longer.

3. Pour in the water and scrape up any bits from the bottom of the inner pot.

4. Add the remaining ingredients and stir.

5. Secure the lid and set the vent to sealing. Manually set the cook time for 8 minutes on high pressure.

6. When cook time is up, let the pressure release naturally for 5 minutes then manually release the remaining pressure.

Tip:

If you don't want it spicy, you can omit the creole seasoning.

Serving Suggestions:

Serve with steamed rice, green onion, sour cream, or shredded sharp cheese.

Six-Can Soup

Audrey L. Kneer, Williamsfield, IL

Makes 8 servings
Prep. Time: 10 minutes • Cooking Time: 3–4 hours • Ideal slow-cooker size: 3½- or 4-qt.

10¾-oz. can tomato soup
15-oz. can whole-kernel corn, drained
15-oz. can mixed vegetables, drained
15-oz. can chili beans, undrained
14½-oz. can diced tomatoes, undrained
14½-oz. can chicken broth

1. Combine all ingredients in slow cooker.
2. Cover. Cook on Low 3–4 hours.

Potato and Corn Chowder

Genelle Taylor, Perrysburg, OH

Makes 6 servings

Prep. Time: 20 minutes ❧ Cooking Time: 3–8 hours ❧ Ideal slow-cooker size: 6-qt.

- 3 cups red potatoes, diced
- 16-oz. pkg. frozen corn
- 3 Tbsp. flour
- 6 cups chicken stock
- 1 tsp. dried thyme
- 1 tsp. dried oregano
- ½ tsp. garlic powder
- ½ tsp. onion powder
- Kosher salt and freshly ground black pepper to taste
- 2 Tbsp. butter
- ¼ cup heavy cream

1. Place potatoes and corn in slow cooker. Stir in flour and toss gently to combine.

2. Stir in chicken stock, thyme, oregano, garlic powder, onion powder, and salt and pepper to taste.

3. Cover and cook on Low for 7–8 hours or High for 3–4 hours.

4. Stir in butter and heavy cream.

5. Serve immediately.

Tip:

Cooking time may need to be adjusted depending on size of diced potatoes.

Soups, Stews, Chilis & Chowders: Meatless

Cream of Broccoli and Mushroom Soup

Leona Miller, Millersburg, OH

Makes 12 servings
Prep. Time: 20 minutes & Cooking Time: 2–5 hours & Ideal slow-cooker size: 5- or 6-qt.

8 oz. fresh mushrooms, sliced
2 lb. fresh broccoli, chopped
3 (10¾-oz.) cans cream of broccoli soup
½ tsp. dried thyme leaves, crushed, *optional*
3 bay leaves, *optional*
1 pint half-and-half
4 oz. extra-lean smoked ham, chopped
¼ tsp. black pepper

1. Combine all ingredients in slow cooker.
2. Cook on Low 4–5 hours or on High 2–3 hours.
3. Remove bay leaves before serving, if using.

Three Bean Chili

Chris Kaczynski, Schenectady, NY

Makes 6 servings
Prep. Time: 10 minutes   Cooking Time: 5 minutes

1 medium onion, diced

16-oz. can low-sodium red kidney beans, drained

16-oz. can low-sodium black beans, drained

16-oz. can low-sodium white kidney or garbanzo beans, drained

14-oz. can low-sodium crushed tomatoes

14-oz. can low-sodium diced tomatoes

1 cup medium salsa

1¼-oz. pkg. dry chili seasoning

1 Tbsp. sugar

1 cup vegetable stock

1. Place all ingredients into the inner pot of the Instant Pot.

2. Secure the lid and set the vent to sealing. Manually set the cook time for 5 minutes on high pressure.

3. When cook time is up, let the pressure release naturally for 10 minutes, then manually release the remaining pressure.

Fix-It and Forget-It Simple & Satisfying

Black Bean Chili

Joyce Cox, Port Angeles, WA

Makes 8 servings

Prep. Time: 20 minutes · Cooking Time: 6–8 hours · Ideal slow-cooker size: 6-qt.

- 1½ cups fresh-brewed coffee
- 1½ cups vegetable broth
- 2 (15-oz.) cans diced tomatoes with juice
- 15-oz. can tomato sauce
- 8 cups cooked black beans, drained
- 1 medium yellow onion, diced
- 4 cloves garlic, minced
- 2 Tbsp. brown sugar, packed
- 2 Tbsp. chili powder
- 1 Tbsp. ground cumin
- Salt to taste

1. Combine all ingredients except salt in slow cooker.

2. Cover and cook on Low for 6–8 hours. Add salt near end of cooking.

Variations:

Use 4 (15-oz.) cans of black beans, rinsed and drained, instead of the 8 cups cooked black beans. Mash some of the beans with a potato masher before adding to cooker. The chili will be thicker.

Serving suggestion:

Great served in bowls with cilantro, cubed avocados, Greek yogurt or sour cream, and grated cheese on top.

Soups, Stews, Chilis & Chowders: Meatless

Main Dishes

Chicken & Turkey

Chicken Cacciatore

Dawn Day, Westminster, CA

Makes 10 servings
Prep. Time: 20 minutes ❧ Cooking Time: 5–6 hours ❧ Ideal slow-cooker size: 3-qt.

2 lb. uncooked boneless, skinless chicken breasts, cubed
½ lb. fresh mushrooms
1 bell pepper, chopped
1 medium-sized onion, chopped
12-oz. can chopped tomatoes
6-oz. can tomato paste
12-oz. can tomato sauce
½ tsp. dried oregano
½ tsp. dried basil
½ tsp. garlic powder
½ tsp. salt
½ tsp. black pepper

1. Combine all ingredients in slow cooker.
2. Cover. Cook on Low 5–6 hours.

Serving suggestions:

- *Serve over rice or pasta.*
- *This would be great served alongside Rosemary Carrots on page 169.*

Salsa Lime Chicken

Maria Shevlin, Sicklerville, NJ

Makes 2–4 servings
Prep. Time: 10 minutes 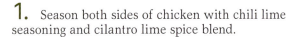 Cooking Time: 17 minutes

4 bone-in chicken thighs, skin on
1 tsp. chili lime seasoning
½ tsp. True Lime Garlic Cilantro Spice Blend
2 tsp. olive oil
1 cup diced onion
1 cup chicken broth
1½ cups of your favorite salsa
1 lime, zested and juiced
2 tsp. garlic powder
2 pkg. True Lime Crystallized Lime Packets
¼ cup brown sugar

Serving suggestion: Slice chicken and serve in a bowl with rice, corn, and black beans. See the front cover photo!

1. Season both sides of chicken with chili lime seasoning and cilantro lime spice blend.
2. Set the Instant Pot to Sauté and let it get hot.
3. Add the olive oil to the inner pot, then sauté the chicken, skin side down, for 3–4 minutes.
4. Turn the chicken over to brown on other side.
5. Add in onion, broth, salsa, lime juice and zest, garlic powder, lime crystals, and brown sugar. Scrape the bottom of the pot and give it a quick stir.
6. Secure the lid and set the vent to sealing. Manually set the cook time for 9 minutes on high pressure.
7. When cook time is up, manually release the pressure.
8. Use two forks to shred the chicken.

Simple Lemon Garlic Chicken

Genelle Taylor, Perrysburg, OH

Makes 4–6 servings
Prep. Time: 10 minutes   Cooking Time: 5–6 hours   Ideal slow-cooker size: 5- or 6-qt.

4–6 boneless, skinless chicken breasts

2 tsp. minced garlic

¼ cup olive oil

1 Tbsp. parsley flakes

2 Tbsp. lemon juice (or juice of 1 whole lemon)

1. Place chicken breasts in slow cooker.

2. Combine garlic, olive oil, parsley flakes, and lemon juice; pour over chicken.

3. Cover and cook for 5–6 hours on Low.

Serving suggestion:

This would be great served alongside Broccoli with Garlic on page 177 or Garlic Butter Cauliflower on page 179.

Main Dishes: Chicken & Turkey   95

Chicken Marsala

Genelle Taylor, Perrysburg, OH

Makes 4 servings
Prep. Time: 10 minutes & Cooking Time: 5½–6½ hours & Ideal slow-cooker size: 5- or 6-qt.

- 4 boneless, skinless chicken breasts
- Salt and pepper to taste
- 2 tsp. minced garlic
- 1 cup sliced mushrooms
- 1 cup sweet marsala cooking wine
- ½ cup water
- ¼ cup cornstarch
- Fresh parsley, roughly chopped

1. Lightly grease slow cooker with nonstick spray.
2. Season chicken with salt and pepper and place in slow cooker.
3. Top chicken with garlic, mushrooms, and wine.
4. Cover and cook on Low for 5–6 hours.
5. Transfer chicken to a plate.
6. Whisk together water and cornstarch; stir into slow cooker.
7. Add chicken back into slow cooker, switch heat to High, cover and cook another 20–30 minutes, until sauce is thickened.
8. Add salt and pepper as needed. Sprinkle with parsley and serve.

Serving suggestion:
This would be great served alongside Best Smashed Potatoes on page 182 and Potluck Baked Corn on page 172.

96 Fix-It and Forget-It Simple & Satisfying

Balsamic Chicken

Hope Comerford, Clinton Township, MI

Makes 4 servings
Prep. Time: 10 minutes ❧ Cooking Time: 5–6 hours ❧ Ideal slow-cooker size: 3-qt.

2 lb. boneless, skinless chicken breasts
2 Tbsp. olive oil
½ tsp. salt
½ tsp. pepper
1 onion, halved and sliced
28-oz. can diced tomatoes
½ cup balsamic vinegar
2 tsp. sugar
2 tsp. garlic powder
2 tsp. Italian seasoning
Cooked pasta for serving

1. Place chicken in crock. Drizzle with olive oil and sprinkle with salt and pepper.

2. Spread the onion over the top of the chicken.

3. In a bowl, mix the diced tomatoes, balsamic vinegar, sugar, garlic powder, and Italian seasoning. Pour this over the chicken and onions.

4. Cover and cook on Low for 5–6 hours.

5. Serve over cooked pasta.

Serving suggestion:

This would be great served alongside Bacon Ranch Red Potatoes on page 185 and Green Beans with Bacon on page 174.

Barbecued Chicken

Charlotte Shaffer, East Earl, PA

Makes 6 servings

Prep. Time: 20 minutes   Cooking Time: 6–8 hours   Ideal slow-cooker size: 3- or 4-qt.

1 lb. frying chicken, cut up and skin removed (organic or free-range, if possible)

10¾-oz. can condensed tomato soup

¾ cup onion, chopped

¼ cup vinegar

3 Tbsp. brown sugar

1 Tbsp. Worcestershire sauce

½ tsp. salt

¼ tsp. dried basil

1. Place chicken in slow cooker.

2. Combine all remaining ingredients and pour over chicken, making sure that the sauce glazes all the pieces.

3. Cover. Cook on Low 6–8 hours.

Serving suggestion:

This would be great served alongside Macaroni and Cheese on page 188 and Corn on the Cob on page 171.

Main Dishes: Chicken & Turkey   99

Chicken Dijon Dinner

Barbara Stutzman, Crossville, TN

Makes 4–6 servings

Prep. Time: 20 minutes   Cooking Time: 4 hours   Ideal slow-cooker size: 6-qt.

2 lb. boneless, skinless chicken thighs
2 cloves garlic, minced
1 Tbsp. olive oil
6 Tbsp. white wine vinegar
4 Tbsp. soy sauce
4 Tbsp. Dijon mustard
1 lb. sliced mushrooms

1. Grease interior of slow-cooker crock.

2. Place thighs in crock. If you need to add a second layer, stagger the pieces so they don't directly overlap each other.

3. Stir together garlic, oil, vinegar, soy sauce, and mustard until well mixed.

4. Gently stir in mushrooms.

5. Spoon sauce into crock, making sure to cover all thighs with some of the sauce.

6. Cover. Cook on Low for 4 hours, or until instant-read meat thermometer registers 160°F when stuck in center of chicken.

7. Serve chicken topped with sauce.

Serving suggestion:

This would be great served alongside Bacon Ranch Red Potatoes on page 185 and Glazed Carrots on page 170.

Main Dishes: Chicken & Turkey   101

Paradise Island Chicken

Rebecca Eldredge, Honolulu, HI

Makes 6 servings
Prep. Time: 15 minutes ❧ Cooking Time: 4 hours
Marinating Time: 4–8 hours, or overnight ❧ Ideal slow-cooker size: 5-qt.

½ cup soy sauce
2 Tbsp. brown sugar
1 tsp. cooking oil
1 tsp. sesame oil
½ cup orange juice
1 large clove garlic, minced
½ tsp. freshly grated ginger root
6 boneless, skinless chicken thighs

1. Mix all ingredients together in bowl except chicken thighs.

2. Pour into heavy plastic bag without holes, big enough to hold the chicken, too. Place thighs in bag. Tie it shut tightly. Swish the bag gently back and forth so all the chicken is covered with the sauce.

3. Place filled bag in large bowl and place in refrigerator for 4–8 hours, or overnight, to marinate meat.

4. Grease interior of slow-cooker crock.

5. Place thighs in cooker. If you need to create a second layer, stagger the pieces so they don't directly overlap each other.

6. Pour the marinade over the thighs, making sure that some of the sauce coats each thigh.

7. Cover. Cook on Low 4 hours, or until an instant-read meat thermometer registers 160°F–165°F when stuck in thighs.

Serving suggestion:
This would be great served alongside Glazed Carrots on page 170 and Quinoa and Black Beans on page 187.

102 ❧ **Fix-It and Forget-It Simple & Satisfying**

Creamy Italian Chicken

Jo Zimmerman, Lebanon, PA

Makes 4 servings
Prep. Time: 15 minutes   Cooking Time: 4 hours   Ideal slow-cooker size: 5-qt.

4 good-sized boneless, skinless chicken thighs
1 pkg. dry Italian salad dressing mix
¼ cup water
8-oz. pkg. cream cheese, at room temperature
10½-oz. can cream of chicken soup
2 cups sliced fresh mushrooms, or 8-oz. can sliced mushrooms, drained

Serving suggestion:

This would be great served alongside Asparagus Bake on page 178.

1. Grease interior of slow-cooker crock.

2. Place thighs in crock.

3. In a bowl, combine salad dressing mix and water. Pour over chicken.

4. Cover. Cook on Low for 3 hours.

5. Meanwhile, beat cream cheese and soup until well blended. Stir in mushrooms.

6. Pour over chicken.

7. Cover. Cook 1 hour longer on Low, or until instant-read meat thermometer registers 160°F–165°F when stuck in center of thighs.

8. Serve over rice.

Main Dishes: Chicken & Turkey

Chicken and Dumplings

Bonnie Miller, Louisville, OH

Makes 4 servings
Prep. Time: 10 minutes • Cook Time: 3 minutes

1 Tbsp. olive oil
1 small onion, chopped
2 celery ribs, cut into 1-inch pieces
6 small carrots, cut into 1-inch chunks
2 cups chicken broth
2 lb. boneless, skinless chicken breast halves, cut into 1-inch pieces
2 chicken bouillon cubes
1 tsp. salt
1 tsp. pepper
1 tsp. poultry seasoning

Biscuits:
2 cups buttermilk biscuit mix
½ cup + 1 Tbsp. milk
1 tsp. parsley

Serving suggestion: This would be great served alongside Potluck Baked Corn on page 172.

1. Set the Instant Pot to the Sauté function and heat the olive oil.

2. Add the onion, celery, and carrots to the hot oil and sauté for 3 to 5 minutes.

3. Pour in the broth and scrape the bottom of the inner pot with a wooden spoon or spatula to deglaze. Press Cancel.

4. Add the chicken, bouillon, salt, pepper, and poultry seasoning.

5. Combine the biscuit ingredients in a bowl until just moistened. Drop 2-Tbsp. mounds over the contents of the inner pot, as evenly spaced out as possible.

6. Secure the lid and set the vent to sealing. Manually set the cook time for 3 minutes.

7. When the cook time is over, manually release the pressure.

Salsa Ranch Chicken with Black Beans

Hope Comerford, Clinton Township, MI

Makes 8 servings
Prep. Time: 10 minutes & Cooking Time: 5–6 hours & Ideal slow-cooker size: 3-qt.

2 large boneless, skinless chicken breasts

1-oz. packet low-sodium taco seasoning

1-oz. packet dry ranch dressing mix

1 cup salsa

10½-oz. can condensed cream of chicken soup

15-oz. can black beans, rinsed and drained

Sour cream, *optional*

Shredded cheese, *optional*

1. Place chicken in crock.

2. In a bowl, mix together the taco seasoning, ranch dressing mix, salsa, cream of chicken soup, and black beans. Pour over the chicken.

3. Cover and cook on Low for 5–6 hours.

4. Serve with sour cream and cheese, if desired.

Serving suggestions:

Serve on top of rice or in a tortilla. This would be great served alongside Corn on the Cob on page 171.

Easy Enchilada Shredded Chicken

Hope Comerford, Clinton Township, MI

Makes 10–14 servings
Prep. Time: 5 minutes • Cooking Time: 5–6 hours • Ideal slow-cooker size: 3- or 5-qt.

5–6 lb. boneless, skinless chicken breast
14½-oz. can petite diced tomatoes
1 medium onion, chopped
8 oz. red enchilada sauce
½ tsp. salt
½ tsp. chili powder
½ tsp. basil
½ tsp. garlic powder
¼ tsp. pepper

Serving suggestions:
Serve over salad, brown rice, quinoa, sweet potatoes, nachos, or soft shell corn tortillas. Add a dollop of yogurt and a sprinkle of fresh cilantro.

1. Place chicken in the crock.
2. Add in the remaining ingredients.
3. Cover and cook on Low for 5–6 hours.
4. Remove chicken and shred it between two forks. Place the shredded chicken back in the crock and stir to mix in the juices.

Instant Pot Adaptation:

1. Place all the ingredients into the inner pot of the Instant Pot.
2. Secure the lid and set the vent to sealing. Manually set the cook time for 10 minutes on high pressure.
3. When cook time is up, let the pressure release naturally for 10 minutes, then manually release the remaining pressure.
4. Remove the lid. Take the chicken pieces out, shred the chicken between two forks, and mix the chicken back into the juices in the pot.

Main Dishes: Chicken & Turkey   107

Traditional Turkey Breast

Hope Comerford, Clinton Township, MI

Makes 6 servings
Prep. Time: 10 minutes • Cooking Time: 35 minutes

7-lb. or less turkey breast
2 cups turkey broth
1–2 Tbsp. olive oil

Rub:
2 tsp. garlic powder
1 tsp. onion powder
1 tsp. salt
¼ tsp. pepper
1 tsp. poultry seasoning

Serving suggestion:

This would be great served alongside Winter Squash with Herbs and Butter on page 180 and Best Smashed Potatoes on page 182.

1. Remove the gizzards from the turkey breast, rinse it, and pat it dry.

2. Place the trivet into the inner pot of the Instant Pot, then pour in the broth.

3. Mix together the rub ingredients in a small bowl.

4. Rub the turkey all over with olive oil, then press the rub onto the turkey breast all over.

5. Place the turkey breast onto the trivet, breast side up.

6. Secure the lid and set the vent to sealing. Manually set the cook time for 35 minutes on high pressure.

7. When the cook time is over, let the pressure release naturally.

Tip:

If you want the breast to have crispy skin, remove it from the Instant Pot and place it under the broiler in the oven for a few minutes, or until skin is as crispy as you like it.

Main Dishes: Chicken & Turkey   109

Turkey Lasagna

Rhoda Atzeff, Lancaster, PA

Makes 8–10 servings
Prep. Time: 20–30 minutes ❧ Cooking Time: 5 hours ❧ Ideal slow-cooker size: 5-qt.

1 lb. lean ground turkey
1 onion, chopped
⅛ tsp. garlic powder
2 (15-oz.) cans low-sodium tomato sauce
6-oz. can low-sodium tomato paste
½–1 tsp. sea salt
1 tsp. dried oregano, or ½ tsp. dried oregano and ½ tsp. dried basil
12 oz. fat-free cottage cheese
½ cup grated Parmesan cheese
12 oz. shredded nonfat mozzarella cheese
12 oz. lasagna noodles, uncooked, *divided*

Serving suggestion:
This would be great served alongside Rosemary Carrots on page 169.

1. Brown ground turkey and onion in skillet. Drain off any drippings.

2. Stir garlic powder, tomato sauce, tomato paste, salt, and herbs into browned turkey in skillet.

3. In a good-sized mixing bowl, blend together cottage cheese, Parmesan cheese, and mozzarella cheese.

4. Spoon ⅓ of meat sauce into slow cooker.

5. Add ⅓ of uncooked lasagna noodles, breaking them to fit.

6. Top with ⅓ of cheese mixture. You may have to use a knife to spread it.

7. Repeat layers two more times.

8. Cover. Cook on Low 5 hours.

9. Allow to stand 10 minutes before serving.

Turkey Slow-Cooker Pizza

Evelyn L. Ward, Greeley, CO
Ann Van Doren, Lady Lake, FL

Makes 8 servings
Prep. Time: 25 minutes ❧ Cooking Time: 3 hours ❧ Ideal slow-cooker size: 6-qt.

1½ lb. 99% lean ground turkey
¼ cup chopped onion
1 Tbsp. olive oil
28-oz. jar fat-free, low-sodium spaghetti sauce
4½-oz. can sliced mushrooms, drained
1–1½ tsp. Italian seasoning, according to your taste preference
12-oz. pkg. wide egg noodles, slightly undercooked
2 cups fat-free, shredded mozzarella cheese
2 cups low-fat, low-sodium, shredded cheddar cheese

1. In a large skillet, cook turkey and onions in olive oil until turkey is no longer pink. Drain.

2. Stir in spaghetti sauce, mushrooms, and Italian seasoning.

3. Spray slow cooker with nonfat cooking spray. Spread ¼ of meat sauce in pot.

4. Cover with ⅓ of noodles. Top with ⅓ of cheeses.

5. Repeat layers twice.

6. Cover. Cook on Low 3 hours. Do not overcook.

Main Dishes: Chicken & Turkey   111

Pork

Pork Baby Back Ribs

Maria Folkerts, Batavia, IL

Makes 6–8 servings
Prep. Time: 20 minutes • Cooking Time: 30 minutes

3 racks of ribs
1 cup brown sugar
1 cup white sugar
1 tsp. garlic powder
1 tsp. garlic salt
1 cup water
½ cup apple cider vinegar
1 tsp. liquid smoke
½ cup barbecue sauce

1. Take the membrane/skin off the back of the ribs.

2. Mix together the remaining ingredients (except the barbecue sauce) and slather it on the ribs.

3. Place the ribs around the inside of the inner pot instead of stacking them. Secure the lid in place and make sure vent is at sealing.

4. Use the Meat setting and set for 30 minutes on high pressure.

5. When cooking time is up, let the pressure release naturally for 10 minutes, then do a quick release of the remaining pressure.

6. Place the ribs on a baking sheet and cover them with the barbecue sauce. Broil for 7–10 minutes (watching so they don't burn).

Serving suggestion: This would be great served alongside Ranch Beans on page 186.

Tip: Placing the ribs around the pot instead of stacking makes it easier.

Main Dishes: Pork 115

Easiest Ever BBQ Country Ribs

Hope Comerford, Clinton Township, MI

Makes 12 servings
Prep. Time: 5 minutes & Cooking Time: 8–10 hours & Ideal slow-cooker size: 6-qt.

4 lb. boneless country ribs

Sea salt and pepper to taste

18-oz. bottle of your favorite low-sugar barbecue sauce

1. Place the country ribs into your crock and sprinkle them with salt and pepper on both sides.

2. Pour half the bottle of barbecue sauce on one side of the ribs. Flip them over and pour the remaining half of the barbecue sauce on the other side of your ribs. Spread it around.

3. Cover and cook on Low for 8–10 hours.

Serving suggestion:

This would be great served alongside Potluck Baked Corn on page 172 and Bacon Ranch Red Potatoes on page 185.

Fix-It and Forget-It Simple & Satisfying

Savory Pork Roast

Mary Louise Martin, Boyd, WI

Makes 4–6 servings
Prep. Time: 15 minutes & Cooking Time: 8–10 hours & Ideal slow-cooker size: oval 6-qt.

4-lb. boneless pork butt roast
1 tsp. ground ginger
1 Tbsp. fresh minced rosemary
½ tsp. mace or nutmeg
1 tsp. coarsely ground black pepper
2 tsp. salt
1 cup water

1. Grease interior of slow-cooker crock.

2. Place roast in slow cooker.

3. In a bowl, mix spices and seasonings together. Sprinkle half on top of roast, pushing down on spices to encourage them to stick.

4. Flip roast and sprinkle with rest of spices, again, pushing down to make them stick.

5. Pour 1 cup water around the edge, being careful not to wash spices off meat.

6. Cover. Cook on Low 8–10 hours, or until instant-read meat thermometer registers 140°F when stuck into center of roast.

Instant Pot Adaptation:

1. In a bowl, mix spices and seasonings together. Sprinkle half on top of roast, pushing down on spices to encourage them to stick.

2. Flip roast and sprinkle with rest of spices, again, pushing down to make them stick.

3. Set the Instant Pot to the Sauté function and heat 1 Tbsp. olive oil. Brown the roast on all sides, about 4 minutes per side. Remove the roast and set it aside momentarily.

4. Pour 1 cup of water into the inner pot and scrape any brown bits off the bottom of the inner pot with a wooden spoon. Press Cancel.

5. Place the roast back into the pot, secure the lid, and set the vent to sealing.

6. Manually set the cook time for 68 minutes on high pressure.

7. When cook time is up, let the pressure release naturally for 10 minutes, then manually release any remaining pressure. Check it with an instant-read meat thermometer. It should register 140°F when stuck into center of roast.

Serving suggestion:

This would go well with Quinoa and Black Beans on page 187 and Rosemary Carrots on page 169.

BBQ Pork Sandwiches

Carol Eveleth, Cheyenne, WY

Makes 4 servings
Prep. Time: 20 minutes · Cooking Time: 60 minutes

- 2 tsp. salt
- 1 tsp. onion powder
- 1 tsp. garlic powder
- 1 Tbsp. olive oil
- 2-lb. pork shoulder roast, cut into 3-inch pieces
- 2 cups barbecue sauce

1. In a small bowl, combine the salt, onion powder, and garlic powder. Season the pork with the rub.

2. Turn the Instant Pot on to Sauté. Heat the olive oil in the inner pot.

3. Add the pork to the oil and turn to coat. Lock the lid and set vent to sealing.

4. Press Manual and cook on high pressure for 45 minutes.

5. When cooking is complete, release the pressure manually, then open the lid.

6. Using 2 forks, shred the pork, pour barbecue sauce over the pork, then press Sauté. Simmer 3 to 5 minutes. Press Cancel. Toss pork to mix.

Serving suggestions:

- *Pile the shredded BBQ pork on the bottom half of a bun. Add any additional toppings if you wish, then finish with the top half of the bun.*

- *Serve alongside Corn on the Cob on page 171 or Potluck Baked Corn on page 172.*

Salsa Verde Pork

Hope Comerford, Clinton Township, MI

Makes 6 servings
Prep. Time: 20 minutes   Cooking Time: 6–6½ hours   Ideal slow-cooker size: 4-qt.

1½-lb. boneless pork loin
1 large sweet onion, halved and sliced
2 large tomatoes, chopped
16-oz. jar salsa verde (green salsa)
½ cup dry white wine
4 cloves garlic, minced
1 tsp. cumin
½ tsp. chili powder

1. Place the pork loin in the crock and add the rest of the ingredients on top.

2. Cover and cook on Low for 6–6½ hours.

3. Break apart the pork with two forks and mix with contents of crock.

Serving suggestion:
Serve over cooked brown rice or quinoa.

Main Dishes: Pork   121

Carnitas

Hope Comerford, Clinton Township, MI

Makes 12 servings
Prep. Time: 10 minutes ❦ Cooking Time: 10–12 hours ❦ Ideal slow-cooker size: 4-qt.

2-lb. pork shoulder roast
1½ tsp. kosher salt
½ tsp. pepper
2 tsp. cumin
5 cloves garlic, minced
1 tsp. oregano
3 bay leaves
2 cups gluten-free chicken stock
2 Tbsp. lime juice
1 tsp. lime zest
12 (6-inch) gluten-free white corn tortillas

1. Place pork shoulder roast in crock.

2. Mix the salt, pepper, cumin, garlic, and oregano. Rub it onto the pork roast.

3. Place the bay leaves around the pork roast, then pour in the chicken stock around the roast, being careful not to wash off the spices.

4. Cover and cook on Low for 10–12 hours.

5. Remove the roast with a slotted spoon, as well as the bay leaves. Shred the pork between 2 forks, then replace the shredded pork in the crock and stir.

6. Add the lime juice and lime zest to the crock and stir.

7. Serve on warmed white corn tortillas.

Instant Pot Adaptation:

1. In a bowl, mix the salt, pepper, cumin, garlic, and oregano. Rub it onto the pork roast.

2. Set the Instant Pot to the Sauté function and heat 1 Tbsp. olive oil. Brown the roast on all sides, about 4 minutes per side. Remove the roast and set it aside momentarily.

3. Pour 1 cup of chicken stock into the inner pot and scrape any brown bits off the bottom of the inner pot with a wooden spoon. Press Cancel.

4. Place the roast back into the pot. Place the bay leaves around the roast and pour in remaining cup of chicken stock.

5. Secure the lid and set the vent to sealing.

6. Manually set the cook time for 30 minutes on high pressure.

7. When cook time is up, let the pressure release naturally for 10 minutes, then manually release the remaining pressure. Check it with an instant-read meat thermometer. It should register 140°F when stuck into center of roast.

Serving suggestion:

Serve over rice and alongside Glazed Carrots on page 170.

Simple Shredded Pork Tacos

Jennifer Freed, Rockingham, AL

Makes 6 servings
Prep. Time: 5 minutes ❧ Cooking Time: 8 hours ❧ Ideal slow-cooker size: 4-qt.

2-lb. boneless pork roast
1 cup salsa
4-oz. can chopped green chilies
½ tsp. garlic salt
½ tsp. black pepper

1. Place all ingredients in slow cooker.

2. Cover; cook on Low 8 hours, or until meat is tender.

3. To serve, use 2 forks to shred pork.

Serving suggestion:
Serve with taco shells and your favorite taco fixings.

Cranberry Jalapeño Pork Roast

Hope Comerford, Clinton Township, MI

Makes 4–6 servings
Prep. Time: 10 minutes & Cooking Time: 7–8 hours & Ideal slow-cooker size: 3-qt.

2–3-lb. pork roast
1 tsp. garlic powder
½ tsp. salt
½ tsp. pepper
1 small onion, chopped
½ jalapeño, seeded and diced
14-oz. can jellied cranberry sauce

1. Place pork roast in crock.

2. Season the pork roast with the garlic powder, salt, and pepper.

3. Dump in the onion and jalapeño.

4. Spoon the jellied cranberry sauce over the top of the contents of the crock.

5. Cover and cook on Low for 7–8 hours.

Serving suggestion:

This would be great served alongside Glazed Carrots on page 170 and Lightened-Up Cheesy Potatoes on page 183.

Main Dishes: Pork 125

Lemon Sweet Pork Chops

Doris Slatten, Mount Juliet, TN

Makes 8 servings
Prep. Time: 15 minutes ❧ Cooking Time: 5–7 hours ❧ Ideal slow-cooker size: oval 7-qt.

8 bone-in, ¾-inch-thick, blade-cut pork chops
¼ tsp. salt
¼ tsp. coarsely ground black pepper
½ tsp. dried oregano
½ tsp. dried chives
⅛ tsp. dried dill
½ tsp. minced garlic
8 lemon slices
4 Tbsp. ketchup
4 Tbsp. brown sugar

Serving suggestion:
This would be great served alongside Glazed Carrots on page 170.

1. Grease interior of slow-cooker crock.

2. In a small bowl, mix the salt, pepper, oregano, chives, dill, and garlic.

3. Sprinkle over both sides of each chop, then lay chop in crock. If you need to make a second layer, stagger the pieces so they don't directly overlap each other.

4. Place lemon slice on each chop.

5. In same small bowl, mix the ketchup and brown sugar. Drop a Tbsp. of mixture on top of each chop.

6. Cover. Cook on Low 5–7 hours, or until instant-read meat thermometer registers 145°F when stuck into center of chops (but not against bone).

Main Dishes: Pork ❧ 127

Barbecued Pork Chops

Loretta Weisz, Auburn, WA

Makes 6 servings
Prep. Time: 10 minutes ❧ Cooking Time: 5–6 hours ❧ Ideal slow-cooker size: 5-qt.

4 loin pork chops, ¾-inch thick
1 cup ketchup
1 cup hot water
2 Tbsp. vinegar
1 Tbsp. Worcestershire sauce
2 tsp. brown sugar
½ tsp. black pepper
½ tsp. chili powder
½ tsp. paprika

1. Place pork chops in slow cooker.

2. Combine remaining ingredients. Pour over chops.

3. Cover. Cook on High 5–6 hours, or until tender but not dry.

4. Cut chops in half and serve.

Serving suggestion:

This would be great served alongside Ranch Beans on page 186.

Paprika Pork Chops and Rice

 INSTANT POT

Sharon Easter, Yuba City, CA

Makes 4 servings
Prep. Time: 5 minutes & Cooking Time: 30 minutes

⅛ tsp. pepper

1 tsp. paprika

4–5 thick-cut boneless pork chops (1 inch to 1½ inches thick)

1 Tbsp. olive oil

1¼ cups water, *divided*

1 onion, sliced

½ green bell pepper, sliced in rings

1½ cups canned no-salt-added stewed tomatoes

1 cup brown rice

Serving suggestion:
This would be great served alongside Garlic Butter Cauliflower on page 179.

1. Mix the pepper and paprika in a flat dish. Dredge the chops in the seasoning mixture.

2. Set the Instant Pot to the Sauté function and heat the oil in the inner pot.

3. Brown the chops on both sides for 1 to 2 minutes a side. Remove the pork chops and set aside.

4. Pour a small amount of water into the inner pot and scrape up any bits from the bottom with a wooden spoon. Press Cancel.

5. Place the browned chops side by side in the inner pot. Place 1 slice onion and 1 ring of green pepper on top of each chop. Spoon tomatoes with their juices over the top.

6. Pour the rice in and pour the remaining water over the top.

7. Secure the lid and set the vent to sealing.

8. Manually set the cook time for 30 minutes on high pressure.

9. When the cooking time is over, manually release the pressure.

Main Dishes: Pork   129

Sausage, Carrots, Potatoes, and Cabbage

Hope Comerford, Clinton Township, MI

Makes 4 servings
Prep. Time: 5 minutes • Cooking Time: 10 minutes

1 Tbsp. olive oil
4 Tbsp. butter
1 large onion, sliced
14-oz. pkg. smoked sausage, sliced
1 cup chicken broth
2 carrots, peeled and chopped
2 lb. red potatoes, chopped
1 small head of cabbage, chopped
1½ tsp. sea salt
1½ tsp. smoked paprika
1 tsp. onion powder
¼ tsp. pepper

1. Set the Instant Pot to the Sauté function and let it get hot. Pour in the oil and butter.

2. Sauté the onion and sausage for about 4 minutes.

3. Pour in the broth and deglaze the bottom of the inner pot, scraping up any stuck-on bits. Press Cancel.

4. Add the remaining ingredients in the order listed.

5. Secure the lid and set the vent to sealing. Manually set the cook time for 6 minutes on high pressure.

6. When cook time is up, manually release the pressure.

Beef

Coca-Cola Roast

Hope Comerford, Clinton Township, MI

Makes 6 servings
Prep. Time: 10 minutes   Cooking Time: 8–10 hours   Ideal slow-cooker size: 6-qt.

3–4 lb. boneless bottom round or flank steak

5–6 small potatoes, cut if you'd like

4–5 medium-sized carrots peeled, cut in half or thirds

2–3 cloves garlic, chopped

Salt and pepper to taste

12-oz. can Coca-Cola

1. Place roast in crock.
2. Place potatoes and carrots around meat.
3. Sprinkle meat and veggies with the garlic, salt, and pepper.
4. Pour the can of Coca-Cola over the top.
5. Cover and cook on Low for 8–10 hours.

Main Dishes: Beef   135

Chuck Roast

Janie Steele, Moore, OK

Makes 6–8 servings
Prep. Time: 20 minutes ❖ Cooking Time: 8 hours ❖ Ideal slow-cooker size: 5-qt.

¼ cup flour
Salt and pepper, to taste
3–4-pound boneless chuck roast
10 pepperoncini, fresh or jarred
2 Tbsp. mayonnaise
2 tsp. apple cider vinegar
¼ tsp. dried dill
⅛ tsp. paprika

1. Mix flour, salt, and pepper and rub into roast. Place roast in crock.

2. Top with pepperoncini.

3. In a small bowl mix mayonnaise, vinegar, dill, and paprika. Spread over meat.

4. Cover and cook on Low for 8 hours. Remove from cooker, shred with forks, and return to cooker. Stir to mix juices and serve.

Serving suggestion:

This would be great served alongside Green Beans Caesar on page 175.

Barbecued Brisket

Dorothy Dyer, Lee's Summit, MO

Makes 9–12 servings
Prep. Time: 10 minutes & Cooking Time: 70 minutes

1 cup beef broth
⅓ cup Italian salad dressing
1½ tsp. liquid smoke
⅓ cup + 2 tsp. brown sugar, packed
½ tsp. celery salt
½ tsp. salt
1 Tbsp. Worcestershire sauce
½ tsp. black pepper
¼ tsp. chili powder
½ tsp. garlic powder
3–4-lb. beef brisket
1¼ cups barbecue sauce
Sandwich rolls

1. Pour the beef broth, Italian dressing, liquid smoke, brown sugar, celery salt, salt, Worcestershire sauce, pepper, chili powder, and garlic powder into the inner pot of the Instant Pot. Stir. Place the brisket into the broth mixture. You may cut it into pieces if needed for it to fit under the broth.

2. Secure the lid and set the vent to sealing. Manually set the cook time for 70 minutes on high pressure.

3. When the cook time is over, let the pressure release naturally.

4. Lift the meat out of the Instant Pot and shred it in a bowl. Pour the barbecue sauce over the meat and stir. Serve on sandwich rolls.

Serving suggestion:

This would be great served alongside Corn on the Cob on page 171.

Main Dishes: Beef   137

Flavorful French Dip

Marcella Stalter, Flanagan, IL

Makes 8 servings
Prep. Time: 5 minutes ❧ Cooking Time: 5–6 hours ❧ Ideal slow-cooker size: 3½-qt.

3-lb. chuck roast
2 cups water
½ cup soy sauce
1 tsp. dried rosemary
1 tsp. dried thyme
1 tsp. garlic powder
1 bay leaf
3–4 whole peppercorns

1. Place roast in slow cooker. Add water, soy sauce, and seasonings.

2. Cover. Cook on High 5–6 hours, or until beef is tender.

3. Remove beef from broth. Shred with fork. Keep warm.

4. Strain broth. Skim fat. Pour broth into small cups for dipping.

Serving suggestions:

Serve beef on French rolls and alongside Rosemary Carrots on page 169.

Hot Beef Sandwiches

Hope Comerford, Clinton Township, MI

Makes 12 servings
Prep. Time: 5 minutes & Cooking Time: 60 minutes

3-lb. rump roast
2 cups beef broth
2 (0.87-oz.) pkgs. beef gravy mix
1 tsp. garlic powder
1 tsp. onion powder
¼ tsp. pepper
6–8 slices of bread

1. Place the roast into the inner pot of the Instant Pot.

2. Mix together the beef broth with beef gravy mix, garlic powder, onion powder, and pepper. Pour it over the roast.

3. Secure the lid and set the vent to sealing. Manually set the cook time for 60 minutes on high pressure.

4. When the cook time is over, let the pressure release naturally.

5. When the pin drops, remove the lid. Remove the beef to a bowl and shred it between 2 forks. Stir it back through the sauce in the inner pot.

6. Serve over slices of bread.

Serving suggestion:
This would be great served alongside Garlic Butter Cauliflower on page 179.

Beef with Broccoli

Genelle Taylor, Perrysburg, OH

Makes 4 servings
Prep. Time: 10 minutes & Cooking Time: 5–6 hours & Ideal slow-cooker size: 5- or 6-qt.

1 cup beef broth
½ cup low-sodium soy sauce
⅓ cup brown sugar
1 Tbsp. sesame oil
3 cloves garlic, minced
1½-lb. boneless beef chuck roast or steak, sliced into thin strips
2 Tbsp. cornstarch
14-oz. bag frozen broccoli florets

1. In a mixing bowl, whisk together the beef broth, soy sauce, brown sugar, sesame oil, and garlic.

2. Lay the beef strips in the slow cooker and pour the sauce over, tossing the strips to coat.

3. Cover and cook on Low for 5–6 hours

4. Remove 4 Tbsp. of the sauce and whisk it in a small bowl with cornstarch. Slowly stir this into slow cooker.

5. Add broccoli. Cook an additional 30 minutes.

Serving suggestion:

Serve over white or brown rice.

Steak and Rice Dinner

Susan Scheel, West Fargo, ND

Makes 8 servings
Prep. Time: 15–20 minutes * Cooking Time: 4–6 hours * Ideal slow-cooker size: 5-qt.

1 cup uncooked wild rice, rinsed and drained
1 cup chopped celery
1 cup chopped carrots
2 (4-oz.) cans mushrooms, drained
1 large onion, chopped
½ cup slivered almonds
3 beef bouillon cubes
2½ tsp. seasoned salt
2 lb. boneless round steak, cut in bite-sized pieces
3 cups water

1. Layer ingredients in slow cooker in order listed. Do not stir.

2. Cover. Cook on Low 4–6 hours.

3. Stir before serving.

Main Dishes: Beef   143

Meatloaf

Hope Comerford, Clinton Township, MI

Makes 6–8 servings
Prep. Time: 10 minutes ❧ Cooking Time: 25 minutes ❧ Standing Time: 10 minutes

2 lb. ground beef
2 eggs
⅔ cup panko breadcrumbs
½ pkg. of dry onion soup mix
1 tsp. garlic powder
1 tsp. salt
½ tsp. pepper
1 cup water

1. Mix all ingredients listed except the water in a bowl.

2. Pour the cup of water into the inner pot of the Instant Pot and place the trivet with handles on top.

3. Spray the inside of a 7-inch baking pan with nonstick spray. Press the meatloaf mixture into the baking pan. Cover the pan with aluminum foil.

4. Place the pan on top of the trivet. Secure the lid and set the vent to sealing.

5. Manually set the cook time for 25 minutes on high pressure.

6. When cook time is up, manually release the pressure.

7. When the pin drops, carefully remove the lid and trivet. Let the meatloaf cool for about 10 minutes before slicing.

Serving suggestion:
Drizzle with ketchup before serving and serve alongside Asparagus Bake on page 178.

Goulash

Janie Steele, Moore, OK

Makes 8–10 servings
Prep. Time: 15 minutes   Cooking Time: 6 hours   Ideal slow-cooker size: 5-qt.

1 lb. extra-lean ground beef
1 pkg. low-sodium taco seasoning
2 cups water
15-oz. can low-sodium diced tomatoes
15-oz. can low-sodium tomato sauce
15-oz. can whole-kernel corn, drained
Salt and pepper to taste
2 cups uncooked elbow macaroni

1. Brown meat in a skillet and drain.
2. Mix remaining ingredients except the macaroni together and pour into slow cooker.
3. Add elbow macaroni, then mix.
4. Cover and cook 6 hours on Low.

Serving suggestion:

This would be great served alongside Green Beans with Bacon on page 174.

Main Dishes: Beef   145

Stuffed Green Peppers

Lois Stoltzfus, Honey Brook, PA

Makes 6 servings
Prep. Time: 20 minutes ❧ Cooking Time: 3–8 hours ❧ Ideal slow-cooker size: 5- to 6-qt.

6 large green peppers
1 lb. extra-lean ground beef, browned
2 Tbsp. minced onion
1 tsp. salt
⅛ tsp. garlic powder
2 cups cooked rice
15-oz. can low-sodium tomato sauce
¾ cup shredded low-fat mozzarella cheese

1. Cut peppers in half and remove seeds.

2. Combine all ingredients except peppers and cheese.

3. Stuff peppers with ground beef mixture. Place in slow cooker.

4. Cover. Cook on Low 6–8 hours, or on High 3–4 hours. Sprinkle with cheese during last 30 minutes.

Walking Tacos

Hope Comerford, Clinton Township, MI

Makes 10–16 servings
Prep. Time: 10 minutes 🌿 Cooking Time: 15 minutes

2 lb. ground beef
2 tsp. garlic powder
2 tsp. onion powder
2 Tbsp. chili powder
1 Tbsp. cumin
1 Tbsp. onion powder
1 Tbsp. garlic powder
1 tsp. salt
½ tsp. oregano
½ tsp. red pepper flakes
1 cup water
10–16 individual-sized bags of Doritos

Suggested Toppings:
Diced tomatoes
Shredded cheese
Diced cucumbers
Chopped onion
Shredded lettuce
Sour cream
Salsa

1. Place the ground beef into the inner pot of the Instant Pot.

2. In a bowl, mix the spices. Sprinkle over the beef. Pour the water around the beef.

3. Secure the lid and set the vent to sealing.

4. Manually set the cook time for 15 minutes on high pressure.

5. When cook time is up, manually release the pressure.

6. When the pin drops, remove the lid and break up the beef with a spoon.

7. To serve, open each bag of Doritos. Crumble the chips in the bag with your hand. Add some of the ground beef, then any additional toppings you desire to each bag. Serve each bag with a fork.

148 **Fix-It and Forget-It Simple & Satisfying**

Sloppy Joes

Hope Comerford, Clinton Township, MI

Makes 15–18 servings
Prep. Time: 25 minutes & Cooking Time: 6–7 hours & Ideal slow-cooker size: 6-qt.

1½ lb. extra-lean ground beef
16 oz. ground turkey sausage
½ large red onion, chopped
½ green bell pepper, chopped
8-oz. can low-sodium tomato sauce
½ cup water
½ cup ketchup
¼ cup tightly packed brown sugar
2 Tbsp. apple cider vinegar
2 Tbsp. yellow mustard
1 Tbsp. Worcestershire sauce
1 Tbsp. chili powder
1 tsp. garlic powder
1 tsp. onion powder
¼ tsp. salt
¼ tsp. pepper

1. Brown the ground beef and sausage in a pan. Drain all grease.

2. While the beef and sausage are cooking, mix together the remaining ingredients in the crock.

3. Add the cooked beef and sausage to the crock and mix.

4. Cover and cook on Low for 6–7 hours.

Serving suggestion:

Serve on hamburger buns and alongside Potluck Baked Corn on page 172.

Main Dishes: Beef   149

Convenient Slow-Cooker Lasagna

Rachel Yoder, Middlebury, IN

Makes 6–8 servings

Prep. Time: 30–45 minutes & Cooking Time: 4 hours & Ideal slow-cooker size: 6-qt.

1 lb. extra-lean ground beef

29-oz. can tomato sauce

8-oz. pkg. lasagna noodles, uncooked, *divided*

4 cups shredded low-fat mozzarella cheese

1½ cups low-fat cottage cheese

1. Spray the interior of the cooker with nonstick spray.

2. Brown the ground beef in a large nonstick skillet. Drain off drippings.

3. Stir in tomato sauce. Mix well.

4. Spread ¼ of the meat sauce on the bottom of the slow cooker.

5. Arrange ⅓ of the uncooked noodles over the sauce. If you wish, break them up so they fit better.

6. Combine the cheeses in a bowl. Spoon ⅓ of the cheeses over the noodles.

7. Repeat these layers twice.

8. Top with remaining meat sauce.

9. Cover and cook on Low 4 hours.

Serving suggestion:
This would be great served alongside Green Beans with Bacon on page 174.

Main Dishes: Beef   151

Spaghetti and Meatballs

Hope Comerford, Clinton Township, MI

Makes 6 servings
Prep. Time: 5 minutes　　Cooking Time: 10 minutes

24 oz. frozen meatballs
8 oz. uncooked spaghetti
14½-oz. can diced tomatoes with basil, garlic, and oregano
3 cups water
24 oz. of your favorite pasta sauce

Serving suggestions:
Serve with grated Parmesan cheese and alongside Broccoli with Garlic on page 177.

1. Pour the meatballs into the inner pot and spread around evenly.

2. Break the pasta in half and place over meatballs in a random pattern to help keep them from clumping all together.

3. Pour the diced tomatoes over the top of the pasta.

4. Pour in the water.

5. Pour in the pasta sauce evenly over the top. Make sure the pasta is completely submerged and push any under that may not yet be covered. DO NOT STIR.

6. Secure the lid and set the vent to sealing.

7. Manually set the cook time for 10 minutes on high pressure.

8. When cook time is up, manually release the pressure.

9. When the pin drops, remove the lid and stir.

Fix-It and Forget-It Simple & Satisfying

Meat Sauce for Spaghetti

Becky Fixel, Grosse Pointe Farms, MI

Makes 6–8 servings
Prep. Time: 20 minutes ❧ Cooking Time: 8 hours ❧ Ideal slow-cooker size: 7-qt.

2 Tbsp. olive oil
28-oz. can crushed tomatoes
28-oz. can tomato sauce
15-oz. can Italian stewed tomatoes
6-oz. can tomato paste
2–3 Tbsp. basil
2 Tbsp. oregano
2 Tbsp. brown sugar
2 Tbsp. garlic paste (or 2 medium cloves, peeled and minced)
2 lb. extra-lean ground sirloin or lean ground turkey

1. Pour olive oil in the crock. Use a paper towel to rub it all around the inside.

2. Add all ingredients except ground sirloin or turkey. Stir together and put slow cooker on Low.

3. In a large skillet, brown your ground sirloin, and drain off any extra grease. Add this to your slow cooker.

4. Cook on Low for 8 hours.

Serving suggestions:

Serve over your favorite pasta and alongside Garlic Butter Cauliflower on page 179.

Meatless & Seafood

Tortellini with Broccoli

Susan Kasting, Jenks, OK

Makes 4 servings
Prep. Time: 10 minutes   Cooking Time: 2½–3 hours   Ideal slow-cooker size: 4-qt.

½ cup water
26-oz. jar your favorite pasta sauce, *divided*
1 Tbsp. Italian seasoning
9-oz. pkg. frozen spinach and cheese tortellini
16-oz. pkg. frozen broccoli florets

1. In a bowl, mix water, pasta sauce, and seasoning together.

2. Pour ⅓ of sauce into bottom of slow cooker. Top with all the tortellini.

3. Pour ⅓ of sauce over tortellini. Top with broccoli.

4. Pour remaining sauce over broccoli.

5. Cook on High 2½–3 hours, or until broccoli and pasta are tender but not mushy.

Cheese Ravioli Casserole

Elizabeth Colucci, Lancaster, PA

Makes 4–6 servings
Prep. Time: 30 minutes & Cooking Time: 2½–3 hours & Ideal slow-cooker size: 3-qt.

10-oz. pkg. cheese ravioli

16-oz. jar spaghetti sauce, with peppers, mushrooms, and onions, *divided*

½ cup Italian breadcrumbs

1 cup mozzarella cheese

¼ cup Parmesan cheese, *optional*

½ cup cheddar cheese

1. Cook ravioli according to package directions. Drain.

2. Spoon enough spaghetti sauce into the slow cooker to cover the bottom. Place ravioli on top.

3. Cover with remaining sauce. Top with bread crumbs. Sprinkle with cheeses.

4. Stir to mix well.

5. Cover and cook on Low 2½–3 hours, or until heated through, but without overcooking the pasta.

Serving suggestion:

This would be great served alongside Broccoli with Garlic on page 177.

Quick-'N'-Easy Meat-Free Lasagna

Rhonda Freed, Lowville, NY

Makes 6 servings
Prep. Time: 10 minutes • Cooking Time: 3–4 hours • Ideal slow-cooker size: 4-qt.

- 28-oz. jar spaghetti sauce, your choice of flavors
- 6–7 uncooked lasagna noodles
- 2 cups shredded mozzarella cheese, *divided*
- 15 oz. ricotta cheese
- ¼ cup grated Parmesan cheese

1. Spread ¼ of sauce in bottom of slow cooker.
2. Lay 2 noodles, broken into 1-inch pieces, over sauce.
3. In a bowl, mix 1½ cups mozzarella cheese, the ricotta, and Parmesan cheese.
4. Spoon half of cheese mixture onto noodles and spread out to edges.
5. Spoon in ⅓ of remaining sauce, and then 2 more broken noodles.
6. Spread remaining cheese mixture over top, then ½ the remaining sauce and all the remaining noodles.
7. Finish with remaining sauce.
8. Cover and cook on Low 3–4 hours, or until noodles are tender and cheeses are melted.
9. Add ½ cup mozzarella cheese and cook until cheese melts.

Serving suggestion:

This would be great served alongside Green Beans with Bacon on page 174.

Main Dishes: Meatless & Seafood

Meatless Ziti

Hope Comerford, Clinton Township, MI

Makes 8 servings
Prep. Time: 10 minutes ❧ Cook Time: 3 minutes

1 Tbsp. olive oil
1 small onion, chopped
3 cups water, *divided*
15 oz. crushed tomatoes
8 oz. tomato sauce
1½ tsp. Italian seasoning
1 tsp. garlic powder
1 tsp. onion powder
1 tsp. sea salt
¼ tsp. pepper
12 oz. ziti
1–2 cups shredded mozzarella cheese

Serving suggestion:

This would be great served alongside Green Beans Caesar on page 175.

1. Set the Instant Pot to the Sauté function and heat the olive oil.

2. When the oil is hot, sauté the onion for 3 to 5 minutes, or until translucent.

3. Pour in 1 cup of the water and scrape any bits from the bottom of the inner pot with a wooden spoon or spatula.

4. In a bowl, mix the crushed tomatoes, tomato sauce, Italian seasoning, garlic powder, onion powder, sea salt, and pepper. Pour 1 cup of this in the inner pot and stir.

5. Pour in the ziti. Press it down so it's in there evenly, but do not stir.

6. Pour the remaining pasta sauce evenly over the top. Again, do not stir.

7. Secure the lid and set the vent to sealing. Manually set the cook time for 3 minutes.

8. When the cook time is over, let the pressure release naturally for 10 minutes, then manually release the remaining pressure.

9. When the pin drops, remove the lid and stir in the shredded mozzarella. This will thicken as it sits a bit.

Vegetable Stuffed Peppers

Shirley Hinh, Wayland, IA

Makes 8 servings
Prep. Time: 20 minutes ⚜ Cooking Time: 6–8 hours
Ideal slow-cooker size: 6-qt. (large enough so that all peppers sit on the bottom of the cooker)

4 large green, red, or yellow bell peppers
½ cup quick-cooking rice
¼ cup minced onion
¼ cup sliced black olives
2 tsp. light soy sauce
¼ tsp. pepper
1 clove garlic, minced
28-oz. can low-sodium whole tomatoes
6-oz. can low-sodium tomato paste
15¼-oz. can corn or kidney beans, drained

1. Cut tops off peppers (reserve) and remove seeds. Stand peppers up in the slow cooker.

2. Mix remaining ingredients in a bowl. Stuff peppers. (You'll have leftover filling.)

3. Place pepper tops back on peppers. Pour remaining filling over the stuffed peppers and work down in between the peppers.

4. Cover. Cook on Low for 6–8 hours, or until the peppers are done to your liking.

5. If you prefer, you may add ½ cup tomato juice if recipe is too dry.

6. Cut peppers in half and serve.

Honey Lemon Garlic Salmon

Judy Gascho, Woodburn, OR

Makes 4 servings
Prep. Time: 15 minutes ☙ Cooking Time: 8 minutes

5 Tbsp. olive oil
3 Tbsp. honey
2–3 Tbsp. lemon juice
3 cloves garlic, minced
4 (3–4-oz.) fresh salmon fillets
Salt and pepper to taste
1–2 Tbsp. minced parsley (dried or fresh)
Lemon slices, *optional*

Serving suggestion:
This would be great served alongside Broccoli with Garlic on page 177.

1. Mix olive oil, honey, lemon juice, and minced garlic in a bowl.

2. Place each piece of salmon on a piece of foil big enough to wrap up the piece of fish.

3. Brush each fillet generously with the olive oil mixture.

4. Sprinkle with salt, pepper, and parsley flakes.

5. Top each with a thin slice of lemon, if desired.

6. Wrap each fillet and seal well at top.

7. Place 1½ cups of water in the inner pot of the Instant Pot and place the trivet in the pot.

8. Place wrapped fillets on the trivet.

9. Close the lid and turn valve to sealing.

10. Cook on Manual at high pressure for 5–8 minutes for smaller pieces, or 10–12 minutes if they are large.

11. When cook time is over, manually release the pressure.

12. Unwrap and enjoy.

Main Dishes: Meatless & Seafood

Shrimp Marinara

Jan Mast, Lancaster, PA

Makes 4–5 servings
Prep. Time: 10–15 minutes   Cooking Time: 6¼–7¼ hours   Ideal slow-cooker size: 4-qt.

6-oz. can low-sodium tomato paste
2 Tbsp. dried parsley
1 clove garlic, minced
¼ tsp. pepper
½ tsp. dried basil
1 tsp. dried oregano
Scant ½ tsp. salt
Scant ½ tsp. garlic powder
28-oz. can low-sodium diced tomatoes, *divided*
1 lb. cooked shrimp, peeled

1. In slow cooker, combine tomato paste, parsley, garlic, pepper, basil, oregano, salt, garlic powder, and half the can of diced tomatoes.

2. Cook on Low 6–7 hours.

3. Turn to High and add shrimp.

4. If you'd like the sauce to have more tomatoes, stir in remaining tomatoes.

5. Cover and cook an additional 15–20 minutes.

Serving suggestion:

Serve over cooked spaghetti squash, garnished with grated Parmesan cheese if you wish.

Main Dishes: Meatless & Seafood   165

Tuna Noodle Casserole

Hope Comerford, Clinton Township, MI

Makes 8 servings
Prep. Time: 10 minutes * Cooking Time: 2 minutes

4 cups chicken broth
1 tsp. sea salt
1 tsp. garlic powder
1 tsp. onion powder
¼ tsp. pepper
12 oz. egg noodles
2 (5-oz.) cans tuna, drained
2 cups frozen peas and carrots, thawed
½ cup heavy cream
3 cups shredded white cheddar cheese

*Serving suggestion:
This would be great served alongside Asparagus Bake on page 178.*

1. Pour the broth, salt, garlic powder, onion powder, and pepper into the inner pot of the Instant Pot. Stir.

2. Pour in the egg noodles and push under the liquid. Sprinkle the tuna on top.

3. Secure the lid and set the vent to sealing.

4. Manually set the cook time for 2 minutes on high pressure.

5. When cook time is up, let the pressure release naturally.

6. When the pin drops, remove the lid and stir in the peas and carrots.

7. SLOWLY stir in the heavy cream, a little at a time, so it does not curdle.

8. Stir in the shredded cheese, a little at a time. Press Cancel.

9. Let the mixture thicken with the lid off until desired thickness is reached. It will thicken as it cools.

Sides

Rosemary Carrots

Orpha Herr, Andover, NY

Makes 6 servings
Prep. Time: 10 minutes   Cooking Time: 2 minutes

1 cup water
1½ lb. carrots, sliced
1 Tbsp. olive oil
½ cup diced green bell pepper
1 tsp. dried rosemary, crushed
¼ tsp. coarsely ground black pepper

Serving suggestion:

This would be great served with Chicken Cacciatore on page 91, Turkey Lasagna on page 110, Savory Pork Roast on page 117, or Flavorful French Dip on page 138.

1. Pour the water into the inner pot of the Instant Pot, place the sliced carrots into a steamer basket, and put the steamer basket into the inner pot.

2. Secure the lid and set the vent to sealing.

3. Manually set the cook time for 2 minutes on high pressure.

4. When the cooking time is over, manually release the pressure. Wait for the pin to drop and remove the lid. Press Cancel.

5. Carefully remove the carrots, set aside, and empty the water out of the inner pot. Wipe dry.

6. Place the inner pot back into the Instant Pot, then press Sauté and heat the oil in the inner pot.

7. Add the green bell pepper and sauté for 5 minutes, then add the carrots and stir.

8. Sprinkle the carrots and green pepper with rosemary and black pepper. Serve and enjoy!

Slow-Cooker Adaptation:

1. Exclude the water.

2. Place all ingredients into the crock of a 2- or 3-qt. slow cooker and stir.

3. Cover and cook on Low for 3–4 hours, or on High for 1½–2 hours.

Sides   169

Glazed Carrots

Beverly Hummel, Fleetwood, PA

Makes 4 servings
Prep. Time: 5 minutes ❧ Cooking Time: 3 hours ❧ Ideal slow-cooker size: 3-qt.

1-lb. bag baby carrots
¼ cup brown sugar
¼ cup water
½ tsp. salt
1 tsp. lemon juice
Chopped fresh parsley, for garnish

1. Combine carrots, brown sugar, water, salt, and lemon juice in slow cooker.

2. Cook on High for 2 hours. Turn heat to Low for another hour, stirring occasionally.

3. Sprinkle with parsley before serving.

Serving suggestion:

This would be great served with Chicken Dijon Dinner on page 101, Paradise Island Chicken on page 102, Cranberry Jalapeño Pork Roast on page 125, Carnitas on page 122, or Lemon Sweet Pork Chops on page 127.

Corn on the Cob

Hope Comerford, Clinton Township, MI

Makes 6 servings
Prep. Time: 10 minutes ⚬ Cooking Time: 2 minutes

1 cup water

6 small ears of corn, husked and ends cut off

1. Place the trivet in the bottom of the Instant Pot and pour in the water.

2. Place the ears of corn inside.

3. Seal the lid and make sure vent is set to sealing. Press Manual and set time for 2 minutes.

4. When cook time is up, release the pressure manually.

Serving suggestions:
- Sprinkle with finely chopped fresh herbs and/or paprika.
- This would be great served with Barbecued Chicken on page 99, Salsa Ranch Chicken with Black Beans on page 106, BBQ Pork Sandwiches on page 118, or Barbecued Brisket on page 137.

Sides

Potluck Baked Corn

Velma Stauffer, Akron, PA

Makes 10–12 servings
Prep. Time: 15 minutes ❧ Cooking Time: 3–4 hours ❧ Ideal slow-cooker size: 6-qt.

3 (12-ounce) bags frozen corn, thawed and drained
4 eggs, beaten
2 tsp. salt
1¾ cups 2% or whole milk
2 Tbsp. melted butter
3 Tbsp. sugar
6 Tbsp. flour

1. Mix all ingredients in mixing bowl until well combined.

2. Pour into greased slow cooker.

3. Cover and cook on High 3–4 hours until set in the middle and lightly browned at edges.

Serving suggestion:

This would be great served with Chicken Marsala on page 96, Chicken and Dumplings on page 104, Easiest Ever BBQ Country Ribs on page 116, BBQ Pork Sandwiches on page 118, or Sloppy Joes on page 149.

Green Beans with Bacon

Hope Comerford, Clinton Township, MI

Makes 6 servings
Prep. Time: 7 minutes   Cooking Time: 5 minutes

5 slices thick-cut bacon, chopped
½ cup chopped red onion
4 cloves garlic, chopped
¾ cup chicken stock
½ tsp. sea salt
⅛ tsp. pepper
⅛ tsp. red pepper flakes
1½ lb. fresh green beans, ends snipped and cut in half

Serving suggestion: This would be great served with Balsamic Chicken on page 98, Goulash on page 145, or Quick-'N'-Easy Meat-Free Lasagna on page 159.

1. Set the Instant Pot to the Sauté function and let it get nice and hot. Spray the inner pot with nonstick cooking spray and then add the bacon. Sauté until crispy.

2. Add the onion and garlic to the inner pot and sauté for an additional 2–3 minutes.

3. Pour in the chicken stock and scrape the bottom of the inner pot with a wooden spoon or spatula, bringing up any stuck-on bits. Press Cancel.

4. Pour in the remaining ingredients.

5. Secure the lid and set the vent to sealing. Manually set the cook time for 5 minutes on high pressure.

6. When the cook time is over, manually release the pressure.

Green Beans Caesar

Carol Shirk, Leola, PA

Makes 6–8 servings
Prep. Time: 15 minutes   &   Cooking Time: 2–3½ hours   &   Ideal slow-cooker size: 3–4-qt.

1½ lb. green beans, ends trimmed
2 Tbsp. olive oil
1 Tbsp. red wine vinegar
1 Tbsp. minced garlic
Salt and pepper to taste
½ tsp. dried basil
½ tsp. dried oregano
¼ cup plain breadcrumbs
¼ cup grated Parmesan cheese
1 Tbsp. butter, melted

1. In slow cooker, combine green beans, olive oil, vinegar, garlic, salt and pepper, basil, and oregano.

2. Cover and cook on High for 2–3 hours, until green beans are as soft as you like them. Stir.

3. Combine breadcrumbs, Parmesan, and butter. Sprinkle over green beans and cook an additional 30 minutes on High with lid off.

Serving suggestion:

This would be great served with Chuck Roast on page 136 or Meatless Ziti on page 160.

Sides   175

Broccoli with Garlic

Andrea Cunningham, Arlington, KS

Makes 4 servings
Prep. Time: 5 minutes • Cooking Time: 2–3 minutes

½ cup cold water
1 head (about 5 cups) broccoli, cut into long pieces all the way through (you will eat the stems)
1 Tbsp. olive oil
2–3 cloves garlic, sliced thin
⅛ tsp. pepper
Lemon wedges to taste

1. Place a steamer basket into the inner pot along with the ½ cup cold water. Put the broccoli into the steamer basket.

2. Secure the lid and set the vent to sealing.

3. Manually set the cook time for 0 minutes on high pressure.

4. Manually release the pressure when it's done. Press Cancel.

5. When the pin drops, open the lid and place the broccoli into an ice bath or run under cold water to stop it from cooking. Let it air dry.

6. Carefully remove the water from the inner pot and wipe it dry.

7. Set the Instant Pot to the Sauté function and heat the oil.

8. Sauté the garlic for 1 minute, then add the broccoli, sprinkle it with the pepper, and continue to sauté for an additional 1–2 minutes.

9. Just before serving, squeeze lemon juice over the top.

Serving suggestion:

This would be great served with Simple Lemon Garlic Chicken on page 95, Spaghetti and Meatballs on page 152, Cheese Ravioli Casserole on page 158, or Honey Lemon Garlic Salmon on page 163.

Sides

Asparagus Bake

Leona M. Slabaugh, Apple Creek, OH

Makes 4–6 servings
Prep. Time: 20 minutes & Cooking Time: 3½–4½ hours & Ideal slow-cooker size: 4-qt.

5 medium potatoes, unpeeled, sliced
1 onion, sliced
1 cup sliced fresh mushrooms
1 bunch fresh asparagus
Salt and pepper
3 Tbsp. butter
½–¾ cup grated smoked cheddar cheese

1. In greased slow cooker, layer potatoes and onion. Sprinkle with salt and pepper. Add mushrooms and asparagus. Sprinkle again with salt and pepper.

2. Dot with butter.

3. Cover and cook on Low for 3–4 hours, until potatoes are tender.

4. Uncover and turn to High. Sprinkle with cheese. Cook uncovered an additional 30 minutes as cheese melts and extra moisture evaporates.

Serving suggestion:

This would be great served with Creamy Italian Chicken on page 103, Meatloaf on page 144, or Tuna Noodle Casserole on page 166.

Garlic Butter Cauliflower

Hope Comerford, Clinton Township, MI

Makes 6–8 servings
Prep. Time: 5 minutes   Cooking Time: 4–5 minutes

1 cup water

1 large head of cauliflower, cut into florets

½ cup butter

4 garlic gloves, crushed

½ tsp. salt

⅛ tsp. pepper

1. Pour the water into the inner pot of the Instant Pot, then place the steamer basket on top.

2. Put the cauliflower florets into the steamer basket.

3. Secure the lid and set the vent to sealing. Manually set the cook time for 1 minute on high pressure.

4. When cook time is up, manually release the pressure. Carefully remove the basket and discard the water from the inner pot. Wipe it dry.

5. Switch the Instant Pot to the Sauté function and let it get hot.

6. Add the butter to the inner pot and let melt. Once melted, add the garlic, cauliflower, salt, and pepper. Sauté for 2–3 minutes.

Serving suggestion:

This would be great served with Paprika Pork Chops and Rice on page 129, Hot Beef Sandwiches on page 140, or Meat Sauce for Spaghetti on page 153.

Sides   179

Winter Squash with Herbs and Butter

Sharon Timpe, Jackson, WI

Makes 6–8 servings
Prep. Time: 30 minutes ❧ Cooking Time: 3–8 hours ❧ Ideal slow-cooker size: 3–4-qt.

3 lb. whole winter squash, mixed kinds, ideally 1 small butternut, 1 small Golden Nugget, 1 small acorn squash

4 Tbsp. butter

4–5 Tbsp. honey

4–8 sprigs fresh herbs, such as tarragon, basil, thyme, and/or rosemary

Salt to taste

1. Peel and halve squash, removing seeds and strings. Cut squash in ¼-inch slices.

2. In lightly greased slow cooker, make layers of squash half-moons, butter, drizzle of honey, and herb sprigs.

3. Cover and cook on High for 3–4 hours or Low for 6–8 hours, until squash is tender.

4. Sprinkle lightly with salt to taste before serving.

Serving suggestion:

This would be great served with Traditional Turkey Breast on page 109.

Best Smashed Potatoes

Colleen Heatwole, Burton, MI

Makes 12 servings
Prep. Time: 30 minutes ❧ Cooking Time: 5–6 hours ❧ Ideal slow-cooker size: 5½-qt.

- 5 lb. potatoes, cooked, peeled, mashed, or riced
- 8 oz. reduced-fat cream cheese, at room temperature
- 1½ cups nonfat plain Greek yogurt, at room temperature
- ¾ tsp. garlic salt or onion salt
- 1½ tsp. salt
- ¼ tsp. pepper
- 2 Tbsp. butter, *optional*

1. Combine all ingredients in slow cooker.
2. Cover. Cook on Low 5–6 hours.

Serving suggestion:

This would be great served with Chicken Marsala on page 96 or Traditional Turkey Breast on page 109.

Lightened-Up Cheesy Potatoes

Hope Comerford, Clinton Township, MI

Makes 8–10 servings
Prep. Time: 10 minutes • Cooking Time: 4–5 hours • Ideal slow-cooker size: 4-qt.

32-oz. bag frozen gluten-free shredded hash browns
1 cup diced onion
8 oz. low-fat shredded cheddar cheese
1 cup nonfat plain Greek yogurt
1 cup nonfat milk
1 cup low-sodium chicken stock
3 oz. reduced-fat cream cheese
1 tsp. garlic powder
1 tsp. onion powder
1 tsp. kosher salt
¼ tsp. ground black pepper

1. Spray crock with nonstick cooking spray.

2. Place all frozen shredded hash browns in crock.

3. In a medium bowl, mix the remaining ingredients. Pour this over the hash browns and mix well in the crock.

4. Cover and cook on Low for 4–5 hours.

Serving suggestion:

This would be great served with Cranberry Jalapeño Pork Roast on page 125.

Sides

Bacon Ranch Red Potatoes

Hope Comerford, Clinton Township, MI

Makes 6 servings
Prep. Time: 15 minutes & Cooking Time: 7 minutes

- 4 strips bacon, chopped into small pieces
- 2 lb. red potatoes, diced
- 1 Tbsp. fresh chopped parsley
- 1 tsp. sea salt
- 4 cloves garlic, chopped
- 1-oz. packet ranch dressing/seasoning mix
- ⅓ cup water
- ½ cup shredded sharp white cheddar
- 2 Tbsp. chopped green onions for garnish

1. Set the Instant Pot to Sauté, add the bacon to the inner pot, and cook until crisp.

2. Stir in the potatoes, parsley, sea salt, garlic, ranch dressing/seasoning, and water.

3. Secure the lid, make sure vent is at sealing, then set the Instant Pot to Manual for 7 minutes at high pressure.

4. When cooking time is up, do a quick release and carefully open the lid.

5. Stir in the cheese. Garnish with the green onions.

Serving suggestion:

This would be great served with Balsamic Chicken on page 98, Chicken Dijon Dinner on page 101, or Easiest Ever BBQ Country Ribs on page 116.

Ranch Beans

Jo Zimmerman, Lebanon, PA

Makes 8–10 servings
Prep. Time: 10 minutes   Cooking Time: 3–4 hours   Ideal slow-cooker size: 3-qt.

16-oz. can kidney beans, rinsed and drained
16-oz. can pork and beans
15-oz. can lima beans, rinsed and drained
14-oz. can cut green beans, drained
12-oz. bottle chili sauce
⅔ cup brown sugar, packed
1 small onion, chopped

1. Combine all ingredients in slow cooker. Mix.
2. Cover and cook on High 3–4 hours.

Serving suggestion:

This would be great served with Pork Baby Back Ribs on page 115 or Barbecued Pork Chops on page 128.

Quinoa and Black Beans

Gloria Frey, Lebanon, PA

Makes 6–8 servings
Prep. Time: 15 minutes ⚜ Cooking Time: 2–3 hours ⚜ Ideal slow-cooker size: 4-qt.

1 onion, chopped
3 cloves garlic, chopped
1 red bell pepper, chopped
1 tsp. olive oil
¾ cup uncooked quinoa
1½ cups vegetable broth
1 tsp. ground cumin
¼ tsp. cayenne pepper
Salt and pepper to taste
1 cup frozen corn
2 (15-oz.) cans black beans, rinsed and drained
½ cup chopped fresh cilantro

1. Sauté onion, garlic, and red bell pepper in olive oil in skillet until softened. Place in 4-qt. slow cooker.

2. Mix quinoa into the vegetables and cover with vegetable broth.

3. Season with cumin, cayenne pepper, salt, and pepper.

4. Cover. Cook on Low for 1 to 2 hours until quinoa is done.

5. Stir frozen corn, beans, and cilantro into cooker and continue to cook on Low for 30–60 minutes until heated through.

Serving suggestion:

This would be great served with Paradise Island Chicken on page 102 or Savory Pork Roast on page 117.

Sides 187

Macaroni and Cheese

Hope Comerford, Clinton Township, MI

Makes 8 servings
Prep. Time: 5 minutes & Cooking Time: 4 minutes

1 lb. uncooked elbow macaroni
2 cups water
2 cups chicken broth
4 Tbsp. butter
1 tsp. salt
½ tsp. pepper
1 tsp. hot sauce
1 tsp. dried mustard
½–1 cup heavy cream or milk
1 cup shredded Gouda
1 cup shredded sharp cheddar cheese
1 cup shredded Monterey Jack cheese

1. Place the macaroni, water, broth, butter, salt, pepper, hot sauce, and dried mustard into the inner pot of the Instant Pot.

2. Secure the lid and set the vent to sealing. Manually set the cook time for 4 minutes.

3. When the cook time is over, manually release the pressure.

4. When the pin drops, remove the lid and stir in the cream, starting with ½ cup. Begin stirring in the shredded cheese, 1 cup at a time. If the sauce ends up being too thin, let it sit awhile and it will thicken up.

Serving suggestion:

This would be great served with Barbecued Chicken on page 99.

Variation:

If you want the mac and cheese to have a crust on top, pour the mac and cheese from the Instant Pot into an oven-safe baking dish. Top with additional cheese and bake in a 325°F oven for about 15 minutes.

Desserts

Caramel Corn

Hope Comerford, Clinton Township, MI

Makes 5–6 servings
Prep. Time: 3 minutes ❧ Cook Time: 15 minutes

2 Tbsp. coconut oil
½ cup popcorn kernels
½ tsp. sea salt

Caramel Sauce:
½ cup sweet cream salted butter
½ cup light brown sugar
2 Tbsp. heavy cream
1 tsp. vanilla extract
¼ tsp. baking soda

1. Set the Instant Pot to the Sauté function. Add the coconut oil and let it melt.

2. When the oil is melted, add the popcorn kernels, stir, then secure the lid. Let it cook for about 3 minutes, or until you do not hear kernels popping.

3. Press Cancel and move the popcorn to a bowl. Toss with the salt.

4. Place the inner pot back into the Instant Pot base and press the Sauté function.

5. Add the butter and let it melt. Once it's melted, add the brown sugar and heavy cream. When the sugar is dissolved add the vanilla and baking soda. Continue to cook until the sauce has thickened into caramel.

6. Press Cancel on the Instant Pot. Add the popcorn back into the inner pot and gently stir to coat it with the caramel sauce.

7. Line a baking sheet with parchment paper, foil, or a silicone mat. Pour the caramel corn onto the baking sheet in a single layer and let it cool.

Desserts

Banana Chocolate Chip Bars

Carol Huber, Austin, TX

Makes 12–15 servings

Prep. Time: 20 minutes ❧ Cooking Time: 2–3 hours ❧ Ideal slow-cooker size: oval 6- or 7-qt.

12 Tbsp. (1½ sticks) butter, softened
⅔ cup granulated sugar
⅔ cup brown sugar
2 eggs
1 tsp. vanilla extract
3 ripe bananas, mashed
2 cups flour
2 tsp. baking powder
½ tsp. salt
12-oz. pkg. semisweet chocolate chips

1. Grease a 9 × 5-inch or 8 × 4-inch loaf pan that will either hang on the edges of your oval slow-cooker crock, or will sit down in the slow-cooker crock on metal jar rings or small trivet.

2. In a good-sized mixing bowl, cream together butter and sugars.

3. Add eggs and vanilla. Mix well.

4. Stir in mashed bananas and stir well.

5. In a medium bowl, sift together flour, baking powder, and salt.

6. Stir dry ingredients into creamed mixture.

7. Stir in chocolate chips.

8. Pour into greased loaf pan.

9. Suspend pan on edges of slow-cooker crock, or place on trivet or jar rings on bottom of crock.

10. Vent slow-cooker lid at one end by propping it open with a wooden spoon handle or chopstick.

11. Cook on High 2–3 hours, or until toothpick inserted in center comes out clean.

12. Uncover pan and remove from cooker. Let cool before slicing into bars.

Brownie Bites

Hope Comerford, Clinton Township, MI

Makes 14 brownie bites
Prep. Time: 5 minutes • Cooking Time: 25–30 minutes

½ cup all-purpose flour
½ cup unsweetened cocoa powder
1 tsp. baking powder
1 cup turbinado sugar
2 eggs
8 Tbsp. (1 stick) butter, melted
1 tsp. vanilla extract
¼ cup + 2 Tbsp. milk
1 cup water

1. Spray 2 silicone egg bite molds with nonstick spray.

2. Mix the flour, cocoa powder, baking powder, and sugar in a bowl.

3. Add the eggs, butter, vanilla, and milk to the dry ingredients and mix well.

4. Evenly divide the batter into the egg bite molds (no more than ⅔ of the way full).

5. Cover each egg bite mold with paper towel and then foil.

6. Place the trivet with handles into the inner pot of the Instant Pot, then pour in the cup of water.

7. Stack the 2 silicone egg molds on top of the trivet in the Inner Pot.

8. Seal the lid and set the vent to sealing.

9. Manually set the cook time for 25–30 minutes, depending on how gooey or firm you like your brownies.

10. When cook time is up, let the pressure release naturally for 10 minutes, then manually release the rest.

11. Carefully remove the trivet with the handles and let the brownie bites sit, uncovered, for about 10 minutes to cool and set before eating or serving.

Gooey Cookie Dessert

Sue Hamilton, Benson, AZ

Makes 8 servings
Prep. Time: 10 minutes ⁂ Cooking Time: 2 hours ⁂ Ideal slow-cooker size: 5-qt.

3½ cups full-fat vanilla ice cream (half of 1.75-qt. container)

16½-oz. roll refrigerator ready-to-bake chocolate chip cookie dough

1. Turn empty slow cooker to High to preheat.

2. Place ice cream in warmed crock, spreading and pushing it to make it a layer. Lumps are fine—they will melt.

3. Slice cookie dough into 12 slices.

4. Press the slices into the ice cream.

5. Cover and cook on High for 2 hours, until edges are browning and the center is cooked.

Tip:

Instead of measuring the ice cream, cut the container in half. It saves the mess of measuring.

Variations:

Use different ice creams and different cookies—there are many flavor options!

Serving suggestion:

Great served warm with whipped cream.

Best Bread Pudding

B. Dennison, Grove City, PA

Makes 8–10 servings
Prep. Time: 10 minutes ❧ Cooking Time: 2–3 hours ❧ Ideal slow-cooker size: 5-qt.

¾ cup brown sugar

6 slices raisin-and-cinnamon-swirl bread, buttered and cubed

4 eggs

1 qt. milk

1½ tsp. vanilla extract

½ tsp. lemon extract, *optional*

1. Spray interior of slow cooker with nonstick cooking spray.

2. Spread brown sugar in bottom of cooker. Add cubed bread. (Do not stir sugar and bread together.)

3. In a mixing bowl, beat eggs well. Beat in milk and vanilla, and lemon extract if you wish. Pour over bread.

4. Cover and cook on High 2–3 hours, or until pudding is no longer soupy. Do not stir. Brown sugar will form a sauce on the bottom.

5. When the pudding is finished, spoon it into a serving dish, drizzling the sauce over top of the bread.

Strawberry Shortcake

Joanna Harrison, Lafayette, CO

Makes 8 servings

Prep. Time: 25 minutes & Cooking Time: 40 minutes & Cooling Time: 7 minutes

1 qt. (4 cups) fresh strawberries
3 Tbsp. honey, *divided*
1½ cups whole wheat pastry flour
1 tsp. baking powder
⅛ tsp. salt
¼ cup butter
2 egg whites
½ cup milk
1 cup water

1. Mash or slice the strawberries in a bowl. Stir in 2 Tbsp. honey. Set aside and refrigerate.

2. In a large mixing bowl, combine the flour, baking powder, salt, and 1 Tbsp. honey.

3. Cut the butter into the dry ingredients with a pastry cutter or 2 knives until crumbly.

4. In a small bowl, beat the egg whites and milk together.

5. Stir the wet ingredients into the flour mixture just until moistened.

6. Pour the batter into a greased 7-inch Bundt pan. Cover tightly with foil.

7. Pour the water into the inner pot and place the trivet on top. Place the Bundt pan on top of the trivet in the inner pot. Secure the lid and set the vent to sealing.

8. Manually set the cook time for 40 minutes on high pressure.

9. When cooking time is up, allow the pressure to release naturally for 10 minutes, then manually release the remaining pressure.

10. When the pin drops, remove the lid and carefully lift the trivet out of the inner pot with oven mitts.

11. Allow cake to cool in the pan for 7 minutes, then remove onto the cooling rack.

12. Cut the cake into desired servings and spoon berries over the top.

Desserts   199

Blueberry Swirl Dump Cake

Phyllis Good, Lancaster, PA

Makes 10–12 servings

Prep. Time: 15–20 minutes ❧ Cooking Time: 3½–4 hours ❧ Ideal slow-cooker size: 5-qt.

3-oz. pkg. cream cheese, softened
18¼-oz. box white cake mix
3 eggs
3 Tbsp. water
21-oz. can blueberry pie filling

1. Grease and flour interior of slow-cooker crock.

2. Beat cream cheese in a large mixing bowl until soft and creamy.

3. Stir in dry cake mix, eggs, and water. Blend well with cream cheese.

4. Pour batter into prepared crock, spreading it out evenly.

5. Pour blueberry pie filling over top of batter.

6. Swirl blueberries and batter by zigzagging a table knife through the batter.

7. Cover. Bake on High 3½–4 hours, or until a tester inserted into center of cake comes out clean.

8. Uncover, being careful to not let condensation from lid drop on finished cake.

9. Remove crock from cooker.

10. Serve cake warm or at room temperature.

Desserts   201

S'mores Lava Cake

Jennifer Freed, Rockingham, AL

Makes 8 servings
Prep. Time: 10 minutes ❧ Cooking Time: 2½–3 hours ❧ Ideal slow-cooker size: 5- or 6-qt.

15¼-oz. box chocolate cake mix, plus ingredients listed on back

3.9-oz. box instant chocolate pudding mix

2 cups cold milk

½ cup mini marshmallows

¼ cup crushed graham crackers

½ cup chocolate chips

1. Grease crock.

2. Prepare cake batter according to package directions directly in crock.

3. In a bowl, prepare the chocolate pudding mix with the 2 cups of milk.

4. Cover cake mix with mini marshmallows in crock, then carefully spread pudding mix over the marshmallows.

5. Top evenly with graham crackers crumbs and chocolate chips.

6. Cover and cook on Low for 2½–3 hours or until edges are done and pudding is bubbly.

Chocolate Pudding Cake

Lee Ann Hazlett, Freeport, IL
Della Yoder, Kalona, IA

Makes 10–12 servings
Prep. Time: 5–10 minutes ❧ Cooking Time: 3–7 hours ❧ Ideal slow-cooker size: 4-qt.

18½-oz. box chocolate cake mix

3.9-oz. box instant chocolate pudding mix

2 cups (16 oz.) sour cream

4 eggs

1 cup water

¾ cup oil

1 cup semisweet chocolate chips

1. Combine cake mix, pudding mix, sour cream, eggs, water, and oil in electric mixer bowl. Beat on medium speed for 2 minutes. Stir in chocolate chips.

2. Pour into greased slow cooker. Cover and cook on Low 6–7 hours, or on High 3–4 hours, or until toothpick inserted near center comes out with moist crumbs.

Desserts

Cherry Cheesecake

Susan Kasting, Jenks, OK

Makes 8 servings
Prep. Time: 7 minutes   Cooking Time: 2 hours   Ideal slow-cooker size: 5-qt.

8 oz. cream cheese
¼ cup sugar
2 (21-oz.) cans cherry pie filling
15¼ oz. yellow cake mix
8 Tbsp. (1 stick) butter, melted

1. Mix cream cheese and sugar.
2. Pour cherry pie filling into greased slow cooker.
3. Top filling with cream cheese mixture, as evenly as possible.
4. Sprinkle cake mix over fillings in crock.
5. Pour butter over cake mix.
6. Cook on Low for 2 hours.

Cherry Pie Crisp

Carrie Fritz, Meridian, ID

Makes 8 servings
Prep. Time: 15 minutes ❧ Cooking Time: 3–4 hours ❧ Ideal slow-cooker size: 3- or 4-qt.

21-oz. can of cherry pie filling
⅔ cup brown sugar
½ cup flour
½ cup old-fashioned oats
1 tsp. vanilla extract
5⅓ Tbsp. (⅓ cup) butter

1. Dump cherry pie filling in a greased slow cooker.

2. In a separate bowl mix together brown sugar, flour, oats, and vanilla. Cut in butter until crumbles form.

3. Sprinkle oat mixture over the cherry pie filling.

4. Cover and cook on Low 3–4 hours. A paper towel can be placed under the lid to help absorb moisture.

Serving suggestion:

Serve warm with vanilla ice cream.

206   Fix-It and Forget-It Simple & Satisfying

Apple Crisp

Carrie Fritz, Meridian, ID

Makes 4 servings
Prep. Time: 15 minutes ❧ Cooking Time: 3–4 hours ❧ Ideal slow-cooker size: 4- or 5-qt.

2 lb. apples
⅔ cup old-fashioned oats
⅔ cup flour
⅔ cup brown sugar
½ tsp. cinnamon
¼ tsp. nutmeg
Pinch salt
6 Tbsp. butter

1. Peel and slice the apples. Place in a greased slow cooker.

2. Combine the rest of the ingredients except for butter in a separate bowl.

3. Cut butter into the rest of the dry ingredients.

4. Sprinkle the topping over the apples.

5. Cook on Low for 3–4 hours.

Serving suggestion:
Serve warm with vanilla ice cream or whipped cream.

Desserts

Peach Crisp

Janie Steele, Moore, OK

Makes 4–6 servings
Prep. Time: 20 minutes   Cooking Time: 4–5 hours   Ideal slow-cooker size: 5-qt.

¼ cup biscuit mix
⅔ cup quick or rolled oats
1½ tsp. cinnamon
¾ cup brown sugar
4 cups canned peaches, cut in chunks
½ cup peach juice

1. Mix biscuit mix, oats, cinnamon, and brown sugar in a bowl.

2. Place peaches and juice in bottom of greased slow cooker.

3. Add dry ingredients over top of peaches.

4. Stir slightly to gently coat peaches.

5. Cook on Low 3½–4½ hours covered, then remove lid for the last 30 minutes.

Serving suggestion:
Serve with ice cream or whipped topping.

Desserts   209

Crockery Apple Pie

Ruthie Schiefer, Vassar, MI

Makes 10–12 servings
Prep. Time: 20 minutes ❧ Cooking Time: 6–7 hours ❧ Ideal slow-cooker size: 4-qt.

8 tart apples, peeled, cored, and sliced
2 tsp. ground cinnamon
¼ tsp. ground allspice
¼ tsp. ground nutmeg
¾ cup milk
2 Tbsp. butter, softened
¾ cup sugar
2 eggs, beaten
1 tsp. vanilla extract
1½ cups biscuit baking mix, *divided*
⅓ cup brown sugar, packed
3 Tbsp. cold butter

1. In large bowl, toss apples with spices. Spoon mixture into lightly greased slow cooker.

2. In separate bowl, combine milk, soft butter, sugar, eggs, vanilla, and ½ cup baking mix. Stir to mix well.

3. Spoon batter over apples.

4. Place remaining baking mix in small bowl. Cut cold butter into it with a pastry cutter until coarse crumbs form.

5. Sprinkle crumbs over batter in slow cooker.

6. Cover and cook on Low for 6–7 hours.

Variation:

I like to use my homemade biscuit mix instead of store-bought:

5 cups all-purpose flour, ¼ cup baking powder, 1 Tbsp. sugar, 1 tsp. salt, 3/4 cup vegetable oil. Mix well. Store in tight container.

—Kelly Bailey

Coconut Rice Pudding

Hope Comerford, Clinton Township, MI

Makes 6 servings
Prep. Time: 2 minutes & Cooking Time: 10 minutes

1 cup arborio rice, rinsed

1 cup unsweetened almond milk

14-oz. can light coconut milk

½ cup water

½ cup turbinado sugar, or sugar of your choice

1 stick cinnamon

¼ cup dried cranberries, *optional*

¼ cup unsweetened coconut flakes, *optional*

1. Place the rice into the inner pot of the Instant Pot, along with all the remaining ingredients.

2. Secure the lid and set the vent to sealing.

3. Using the Porridge setting, set the cook time for 10 minutes.

4. When the cooking time is over, let the pressure release naturally.

5. When the pin drops, remove the lid and remove cinnamon stick.

6. Stir and serve as is or sprinkle some cranberries and unsweetened coconut flakes on top of each serving. Enjoy!

Slow-Cooker Adaptation:

1. Spray 5–6-qt. crock with nonstick spray.

2. In crock, whisk together the milk, coconut milk, and sugar.

3. Add in the rice and cinnamon stick.

4. Cover and cook on Low about 2–2½ hours, or until rice is tender and the pudding has thickened.

5. Remove cinnamon stick.

6. Stir and serve as is or sprinkle some cranberries and unsweetened coconut flakes on top of each serving. Enjoy!

Desserts 211

Buttery Rice Pudding

Janie Steele, Moore, OK

Makes 6–8 servings
Prep. Time: 5 minutes & Cooking Time: 14 minutes

1½ Tbsp. butter
1 cup uncooked rice
½ cup sugar
1 cup water
2 cups milk (2% works best)
1 egg
¼ cup evaporated milk
½ tsp. vanilla extract
½ tsp. almond extract, *optional*
Nutmeg, *optional*
Cinnamon, *optional*

1. In the inner pot of the Instant Pot, melt butter using the Sauté setting. Add the rice, sugar, water, and milk, and stir.

2. Secure lid and make sure vent is at sealing. Cook on Manual on high pressure for 14 minutes. Let the pressure release naturally when cook time is up.

3. In a bowl whisk together the egg and evaporated milk.

4. Take a spoonful of rice mixture and add slowly to egg mixture.

5. Return all to the inner pot and stir in the vanilla and optional almond extract.

6. Use the Sauté function and bring mixture to bubble for 30–60 seconds.

7. Stir slowly so it does not stick to the pot.

8. Use nutmeg or cinnamon to garnish if desired.

Metric Equivalent Measurements

If you're accustomed to using metric measurements, I don't want you to be inconvenienced by the imperial measurements I use in this book.

Use this handy chart, too, to figure out the size of the slow cooker you'll need for each recipe.

Weight (Dry Ingredients)

1 oz		30 g
4 oz	¼ lb	120 g
8 oz	½ lb	240 g
12 oz	¾ lb	360 g
16 oz	1 lb	480 g
32 oz	2 lb	960 g

Slow-Cooker Sizes

1-quart	0.96 l
2-quart	1.92 l
3-quart	2.88 l
4-quart	3.84 l
5-quart	4.80 l
6-quart	5.76 l
7-quart	6.72 l
8-quart	7.68 l

Volume (Liquid Ingredients)

½ tsp.		2 ml
1 tsp.		5 ml
1 Tbsp.	½ fl oz	15 ml
2 Tbsp.	1 fl oz	30 ml
¼ cup	2 fl oz	60 ml
⅓ cup	3 fl oz	80 ml
½ cup	4 fl oz	120 ml
⅔ cup	5 fl oz	160 ml
¾ cup	6 fl oz	180 ml
1 cup	8 fl oz	240 ml
1 pt	16 fl oz	480 ml
1 qt	32 fl oz	960 ml

Length

¼ in	6 mm
½ in	13 mm
¾ in	19 mm
1 in	25 mm
6 in	15 cm
12 in	30 cm

Recipe & Ingredient Index

A

allspice
  Crockery Apple Pie, 210
  Overnight French Toast, 31
almonds
  Steak and Rice Dinner, 143
Apple Cinnamon Oatmeal, 38
Apple Crisp, 207
apples
  Apple Cinnamon Oatmeal, 38
  Crockery Apple Pie, 210
  dried
    Overnight Oat Groats, 35
apricots
  Overnight Steel Cut Oatmeal, 34
Asparagus Bake, 178

B

bacon
  Canadian
    Potato-Bacon Gratin, 29
    Split Pea Soup, 58
  Creamy Potato Chowder, 61
  Easy Quiche, 16
  Green Beans with Bacon, 174
  Kelly's Company Omelette, 19
  Potato Soup, 59
Bacon Ranch Red Potatoes, 185
Balsamic Chicken, 98
Banana Chocolate Chip Bars, 194
Barbecued Brisket, 137
Barbecued Chicken, 99
Barbecued Pork Chops, 128
barbecue sauce
  Barbecued Brisket, 137
  BBQ Pork Sandwiches, 118
  Easiest Ever BBQ Country Ribs, 116
  Pork Baby Back Ribs, 115
barley
  Beef Mushroom Barley Soup, 66
basil
  Barbecued Chicken, 99
  Best Bean and Ham Soup, 54
  Chicken Cacciatore, 91
  Chicken Noodle Soup, 43
  Green Beans Caesar, 175
  Kelly's Company Omelette, 19
  Meat Sauce for Spaghetti, 153
  Shrimp Marinara, 165
  Super Healthy Cabbage Soup, 76
  Winter Squash with Herbs and Butter, 180
bay leaves
  Best Bean and Ham Soup, 54
  Carnitas, 122
  Chicken Stew, 48
  Cream of Broccoli and Mushroom Soup, 83
  Flavorful French Dip, 138
BBQ Pork Sandwiches, 118
beans
  baked
    Ham and Bean Stew, 55
  black
    Black Bean Chili, 85
    Black Bean Soup with Chicken and Salsa, 46
    Easy Chicken Tortilla Soup, 45
    Quinoa and Black Beans, 187
    Salsa Ranch Chicken with Black Beans, 106
    Spicy Black Bean Sweet Potato Stew, 78
    Three Bean Chili, 84
  cannellini
    Italian Shredded Pork Stew, 53
    Tuscan Beef Stew, 69
    White Chicken Chili, 49
  chili
    Six-Can Soup, 80
  garbanzo
    White Chicken Chili, 49
  green
    Green Beans Caesar, 175
    Green Beans with Bacon, 174
    Kielbasa Soup, 56
    Ranch Beans, 186
  kidney
    Chili Comerford-Style, 71
    Chipotle Beef Chili, 72
    Ranch Beans, 186
    Vegetable Stuffed Peppers, 162
    Veggie Minestrone, 75
  lentils
    Mediterranean Lentil Soup, 77
  navy
    Best Bean and Ham Soup, 54
  pork and beans
    Ranch Beans, 186
  red kidney
    Three Bean Chili, 84
  white kidney
    Italian Shredded Pork Stew, 53
    Three Bean Chili, 84
beef
  Chipotle Beef Chili, 72

chuck roast
    Beef with Broccoli, 141
    Chuck Roast, 136
    Flavorful French Dip, 138
flank
    Coca-Cola Roast, 135
ground, 153
    Convenient Slow-Cooker Lasagna, 151
    Goulash, 145
    Meatloaf, 144
    Sloppy Joes, 149
    Stuffed Green Peppers, 146
    Walking Tacos, 148
round steak
    Steak and Rice Dinner, 143
rump roast
    Hot Beef Sandwiches, 140
    Tuscan Beef Stew, 69
Beef Mushroom Barley Soup, 66
Beef Stew, 68
Beef Vegetable Soup, 65
Beef with Broccoli, 141
bell pepper
    Breakfast for Dinner Casserole, 23
    Egg Bites, 15
    Fiesta Hashbrowns, 27
    Italian Sausage and Sweet Pepper Hash, 30
    Overnight Mexican Breakfast Casserole, 26
    Paprika Pork Chops and Rice, 129
    Quinoa and Black Beans, 187
    Rosemary Carrots, 169
    Sloppy Joes, 149
    Stuffed Green Peppers, 146
    Vegetable Stuffed Peppers, 162
    White Chicken Chili, 49

Best Bean and Ham Soup, 54
Best Bread Pudding, 198
Best Smashed Potatoes, 182
biscuits
    Chicken and Dumplings, 104
Black Bean Chili, 85
Black Bean Soup with Chicken and Salsa, 46
Blueberry Swirl Dump Cake, 201
bread
    Barbecued Brisket, 137
    Cinnamon French Toast Casserole, 32
    Hot Beef Sandwiches, 140
    Overnight French Toast, 31
    raisin cinnamon swirl
        Best Bread Pudding, 198
breadcrumbs
    Cheese Ravioli Casserole, 158
    Green Beans Caesar, 175
    Meatloaf, 144
breakfast
    Apple Cinnamon Oatmeal, 38
    Breakfast Burrito Casserole, 24
    Breakfast for Dinner Casserole, 23
    Cinnamon French Toast Casserole, 32
    Easy Quiche, 16
    Egg Bites, 15
    Fiesta Hashbrowns, 27
    German Chocolate Oatmeal, 37
    Italian Sausage and Sweet Pepper Hash, 30
    Kelly's Company Omelette, 19
    Overnight French Toast, 31
    Overnight Mexican Breakfast Casserole, 26
    Overnight Oat Groats, 35

    Overnight Steel-Cut Oatmeal, 34
    Potato-Bacon Gratin, 29
    Southwestern Egg Casserole, 20
Breakfast Burrito Casserole, 24
Breakfast for Dinner Casserole, 23
brisket
    Barbecued Brisket, 137
broccoli
    Beef with Broccoli, 141
    Cream of Broccoli and Mushroom Soup, 83
    Egg Bites, 15
    Tortellini with Broccoli, 157
Broccoli with Garlic, 177
Brownie Bites, 195
Buttery Rice Pudding, 212

C
cabbage
    Kielbasa Soup, 56
    Sausage, Carrots, Potatoes and Cabbage, 130
    Super Healthy Cabbage Soup, 76
cake
    Blueberry Swirl Dump Cake, 201
    Cherry Cheesecake, 204
    Chocolate Pudding Cake, 203
    S'mores Lava Cake, 202
    Strawberry Shortcake, 199
Caramel Corn, 193
Carnitas, 122
carrots
    Glazed Carrots, 170
    Rosemary Carrots, 169
casserole
    Breakfast Burrito Casserole, 24
    Breakfast for Dinner Casserole, 23

Cinnamon French Toast
  Casserole, 32
Overnight Mexican
  Breakfast Casserole, 26
Southwestern Egg
  Casserole, 20
cauliflower
  Garlic Butter Cauliflower,
    179
cayenne
  Breakfast for Dinner
    Casserole, 23
  Kelly's Company Omelette,
    19
  Quinoa and Black Beans,
    187
  White Chicken Chili, 49
cheese
  cheddar
    Asparagus Bake, 178
    Bacon Ranch Red
      Potatoes, 185
    Breakfast for Dinner
      Casserole, 23
    Cheese Ravioli Casserole,
      158
    Easy Quiche, 16
    Egg Bites, 15
    Kelly's Company
      Omelette, 19
    Lightened-Up Cheesy
      Potatoes, 183
    Macaroni and Cheese,
      188
    Overnight Mexican
      Breakfast Casserole, 26
    Southwestern Egg
      Casserole, 20
    Tuna Noodle Casserole,
      166
    Turkey Slow-Cooker
      Pizza, 111
    White Chicken Chili, 49
  cottage
    Convenient Slow-Cooker
      Lasagna, 151

  Southwestern Egg
    Casserole, 20
  Turkey Lasagna, 110
cream
  Best Smashed Potatoes,
    182
  Blueberry Swirl Dump
    Cake, 201
  Cherry Cheesecake, 204
  Creamy Italian Chicken,
    103
  Creamy Potato Chowder,
    61
  Lightened-Up Cheesy
    Potatoes, 183
  Easy Chicken Tortilla Soup,
    45
  Gouda
    Macaroni and Cheese,
      188
  Mediterranean Lentil Soup,
    77
  Mexican blend
    Breakfast Burrito
      Casserole, 24
  Monterey Jack
    Fiesta Hashbrowns, 27
    Macaroni and Cheese,
      188
  mozzarella
    Cheese Ravioli Casserole,
      158
    Convenient Slow-Cooker
      Lasagna, 151
    Meatless Ziti, 160
    Quick-'N'-Easy Meat-Free
      Lasagna, 159
    Stuffed Green Peppers,
      146
    Turkey Lasagna, 110
    Turkey Slow-Cooker
      Pizza, 111
  Parmesan
    Cheese Ravioli Casserole,
      158
    Green Beans Caesar, 175

  Quick-'N'-Easy Meat-Free
    Lasagna, 159
  Turkey Lasagna, 110
  Veggie Minestrone, 75
  pepper jack
    Breakfast for Dinner
      Casserole, 23
  ricotta
    Quick-'N'-Easy Meat-Free
      Lasagna, 159
    Salsa Ranch Chicken with
      Black Beans, 106
  Swiss
    Italian Sausage and Sweet
      Pepper Hash, 30
    Potato-Bacon Gratin, 29
cheesecake
  Cherry Cheesecake, 204
  Cheese Ravioli Casserole, 158
  Cherry Cheesecake, 204
  Cherry Pie Crisp, 206
chicken
  breasts
    Balsamic Chicken, 98
    Black Bean Soup with
      Chicken and Salsa, 46
    Chicken and Corn Soup,
      44
    Chicken and Dumplings,
      104
    Chicken Marsala, 96
    Chicken Stew, 48
    Easy Chicken Tortilla
      Soup, 45
    Easy Enchilada Shredded
      Chicken, 107
    Salsa Ranch Chicken
      with Black Beans, 106
    Simple Lemon Garlic
      Chicken, 92
  frying
    Barbecued Chicken, 99
  thighs
    Chicken Dijon Dinner, 101
    Creamy Italian Chicken,
      103

Recipe & Ingredient Index   217

Paradise Island Chicken, 102
Salsa Lime Chicken, 92
White Chicken Chili, 49
Chicken and Corn Soup, 44
Chicken and Dumplings, 104
Chicken Cacciatore, 91
Chicken Dijon Dinner, 101
Chicken Marsala, 96
Chicken Noodle Soup, 43
Chicken Stew, 48
chili
   Black Bean Chili, 85
   Chipotle Beef Chili, 72
   Three Bean Chili, 84
   White Chicken Chili, 49
Chili Comerford-Style, 71
chili powder
   Barbecued Pork Chops, 128
   Black Bean Chili, 85
   Chili Comerford-Style, 71
   Chipotle Beef Chili, 72
   Easy Enchilada Shredded Chicken, 107
   Sloppy Joes, 149
   Three Bean Chili, 84
   Walking Tacos, 148
chili sauce
   Ranch Beans, 186
Chipotle Beef Chili, 72
chocolate chips
   Banana Chocolate Chip Bars, 194
   Chocolate Pudding Cake, 203
   S'mores Lava Cake, 202
Chocolate Pudding Cake, 203
Chuck Roast, 136
cilantro
   Quinoa and Black Beans, 187
cinnamon
   Apple Cinnamon Oatmeal, 38
   Apple Crisp, 207

   Cinnamon French Toast Casserole, 32
   Coconut Rice Pudding, 211, 212
   Crockery Apple Pie, 210
   Overnight French Toast, 31
   Overnight Oat Groats, 35
   Peach Crisp, 209
Cinnamon French Toast Casserole, 32
Coca-Cola Roast, 135
cocoa powder
   Brownie Bites, 195
   German Chocolate Oatmeal, 37
coconut
   Coconut Rice Pudding, 211
   German Chocolate Oatmeal, 37
coconut milk
   German Chocolate Oatmeal, 37
Coconut Rice Pudding, 211
coffee
   Black Bean Chili, 85
Convenient Slow-Cooker Lasagna, 151
cookie dough
   chocolate chip
      Gooey Cookie Dessert, 196
corn
   Black Bean Soup with Chicken and Salsa, 46
   Chicken and Corn Soup, 44
   cream-style
      Chicken and Corn Soup, 44
   Goulash, 145
   Potato and Corn Chowder, 81
   Potluck Baked Corn, 172
   Quinoa and Black Beans, 187
   Six-Can Soup, 80
   Vegetable Stuffed Peppers, 162

Corn on the Cob, 171
cranberries
   dried
      Coconut Rice Pudding, 211
      Overnight Steel-Cut Oatmeal, 34
Cranberry Jalapeño Pork Roast, 125
cranberry sauce
   Cranberry Jalapeño Pork Roast, 125
cream
   Caramel Corn, 193
   Cream of Broccoli and Mushroom Soup, 83
   Potato and Corn Chowder, 81
   Potato Soup, 59
   Tuna Noodle Casserole, 166
Cream of Broccoli and Mushroom Soup, 83
cream of chicken soup
   Creamy Italian Chicken, 103
   Creamy Potato Chowder, 61
cream of tomato soup
   Chili Comerford-Style, 71
Creamy Italian Chicken, 103
Creamy Potato Chowder, 61
creole seasoning
   Spicy Black Bean Sweet Potato Stew, 78
Crockery Apple Pie, 210
cumin
   Black Bean Chili, 85
   Black Bean Soup with Chicken and Salsa, 46
   Carnitas, 122
   Quinoa and Black Beans, 187
   Salsa Verde Pork, 121
   Spicy Black Bean Sweet Potato Stew, 78
   Walking Tacos, 148
   White Chicken Chili, 49

D

desserts
   Apple Crisp, 207
   Banana Chocolate Chip
      Bars, 194
   Best Bread Pudding, 198
   Blueberry Swirl Dump
      Cake, 201
   Brownie Bites, 195
   Caramel Corn, 193
   Cherry Cheesecake, 204
   Cherry Pie Crisp, 206
   Chocolate Pudding Cake,
      203
   Coconut Rice Pudding, 211,
      212
   Crockery Apple Pie, 210
   Gooey Cookie Dessert, 196
   Peach Crisp, 209
   S'mores Lava Cake, 202
   Strawberry Shortcake, 199
dill
   Lemon Sweet Pork Chops,
      127
Doritos
   Walking Tacos, 148
dumplings
   Chicken and Dumplings,
      104

E

Easiest Ever BBQ Country
   Ribs, 116
Easy Chicken Tortilla Soup, 45
Easy Enchilada Shredded
   Chicken, 107
Easy Quiche, 16
Egg Bites, 15
eggs
   Cinnamon French Toast
      Casserole, 32
   Overnight French Toast, 31
   Potluck Baked Corn, 172
enchilada sauce
   Easy Enchilada Shredded
      Chicken, 107

F

Fiesta Hashbrowns, 27
Flavorful French Dip, 138

G

Garlic Butter Cauliflower, 179
German Chocolate Oatmeal,
   37
ginger
   Paradise Island Chicken,
      102
   Savory Pork Roast, 117
Glazed Carrots, 170
Gooey Cookie Dessert, 196
Goulash, 145
graham crackers
   S'mores Lava Cake, 202
Green Beans Caesar, 175
Green Beans with Bacon, 174
green chilies
   Easy Chicken Tortilla Soup,
      45
   Overnight Mexican
      Breakfast Casserole, 26
   Simple Shredded Pork
      Tacos, 124
   Southwestern Egg
      Casserole, 20
groats
   Overnight Oat Groats, 35

H

ham
   Cream of Broccoli and
      Mushroom Soup, 83
   Easy Quiche, 16
   Kelly's Company Omelette,
      19
Ham and Bean Stew, 55
ham bone
   Best Bean and Ham Soup, 54
honey
   Honey Lemon Garlic
      Salmon, 163
   Winter Squash with Herbs
      and Butter, 180

Honey Lemon Garlic Salmon,
   163
Hot Beef Sandwiches, 140
hot sauce
   Egg Bites, 15
   Macaroni and Cheese, 188

I

ice cream
   vanilla
      Gooey Cookie Dessert,
         196
Instant Pot
   Bacon Ranch Red Potatoes,
      185
   Barbecued Brisket, 137
   BBQ Pork Sandwiches, 118
   Beef Mushroom Barley
      Soup, 66
   Best Bean and Ham Soup,
      54
   Breakfast Burrito Casserole,
      24
   Breakfast for Dinner
      Casserole, 23
   Broccoli with Garlic, 177
   Brownie Bites, 195
   Caramel Corn, 193
   Carnitas, 122
   Chicken and Dumplings,
      104
   Chicken Noodle Soup, 43
   Chicken Stew, 48
   Chili Comerford-Style, 71
   Cinnamon French Toast
      Casserole, 32
   Coconut Rice Pudding, 211,
      212
   Corn on the Cob, 171
   Easy Enchilada Shredded
      Chicken, 107
   Easy Quiche, 16
   Egg Bites, 15
   Garlic Butter Cauliflower,
      179
   Green Beans with Bacon, 174

Recipe & Ingredient Index

Honey Lemon Garlic
   Salmon, 163
Hot Beef Sandwiches, 140
Macaroni and Cheese, 188
Meatless Ziti, 160
Meatloaf, 144
Mediterranean Lentil Soup,
   77
Paprika Pork Chops and
   Rice, 129
Pork Baby Back Ribs, 115
Potato-Bacon Gratin, 29
Potato Soup, 59
Rosemary Carrots, 169
Salsa Lime Chicken, 92
Sausage, Carrots, Potatoes
   and Cabbage, 130
Savory Pork Roast, 117
Southwestern Egg
   Casserole, 20
Spaghetti and Meatballs, 152
Spicy Black Bean Sweet
   Potato Stew, 78
Strawberry Shortcake, 199
Super Healthy Cabbage
   Soup, 76
Three Bean Chili, 84
Traditional Turkey Breast,
   109
Tuna Noodle Casserole, 166
Veggie Minestrone, 75
Walking Tacos, 148
Italian dressing
   Barbecued Brisket, 137
Italian dressing mix
   Creamy Italian Chicken, 103
Italian Sausage and Sweet
   Pepper Hash, 30
Italian seasoning
   Balsamic Chicken, 98
   Chicken Stew, 48
   Meatless Ziti, 160
   Tortellini with Broccoli, 157
   Turkey Slow-Cooker Pizza,
      111
   Tuscan Beef Stew, 69

Italian Shredded Pork Stew, 53

J
jalapeño
   Black Bean Soup with
      Chicken and Salsa, 46
   Cranberry Jalapeño Pork
      Roast, 125
   Super Healthy Cabbage
      Soup, 76

K
kale
   Italian Shredded Pork Stew,
      53
Kelly's Company Omelette, 19
ketchup
   Barbecued Pork Chops, 128
   Beef Stew, 68
   Lemon Sweet Pork Chops,
      127
   Sloppy Joes, 149
Kielbasa Soup, 56

L
lasagna
   Convenient Slow-Cooker
      Lasagna, 151
   Quick-'N'-Easy Meat-Free
      Lasagna, 159
   Turkey Lasagna, 110
Lemon Sweet Pork Chops, 127
lentils
   Mediterranean Lentil Soup,
      77
Lightened-Up Cheesy
   Potatoes, 183
liquid smoke
   Pork Baby Back Ribs, 115

M
Macaroni and Cheese, 188
mace
   Savory Pork Roast, 117
marjoram
   Mediterranean Lentil Soup,
      77

marshmallows
   S'mores Lava Cake, 202
mayonnaise
   Chuck Roast, 136
meatballs
   Spaghetti and Meatballs,
      152
Meatless Ziti, 160
Meatloaf, 144
Meat Sauce for Spaghetti, 153
Mediterranean Lentil Soup, 77
mushrooms
   Asparagus Bake, 178
   Beef Mushroom Barley
      Soup, 66
   Black Bean Soup with
      Chicken and Salsa, 46
   Chicken Cacciatore, 91
   Chicken Dijon Dinner, 101
   Chicken Marsala, 96
   Cream of Broccoli and
      Mushroom Soup, 83
   Creamy Italian Chicken,
      103
   Easy Quiche, 16
   Fiesta Hashbrowns, 27
   Kelly's Company Omelette,
      19
   Steak and Rice Dinner, 143
   Turkey Slow-Cooker Pizza,
      111
mustard
   Dijon
      Chicken Dijon Dinner,
         101
   dried
      Macaroni and Cheese,
         188
   Sloppy Joes, 149

N
noodles
   Balsamic Chicken, 98
   Cheese Ravioli Casserole,
      158
   Chicken Noodle Soup, 43

Convenient Slow-Cooker
  Lasagna, 151
Goulash, 145
Macaroni and Cheese, 188
Meatless Ziti, 160
Quick-'N'-Easy Meat-Free
  Lasagna, 159
Tortellini with Broccoli, 157
Tuna Noodle Casserole, 166
Turkey Slow-Cooker Pizza,
  111
Veggie Minestrone, 75
nutmeg
  Apple Crisp, 207
  Best Bean and Ham Soup,
    54
  Coconut Rice Pudding, 212
  Crockery Apple Pie, 210
  Savory Pork Roast, 117

O
oats
  Apple Cinnamon Oatmeal,
    38
  Apple Crisp, 207
  Cherry Pie Crisp, 206
  German Chocolate
    Oatmeal, 37
  Overnight Steel-Cut
    Oatmeal, 34
  Peach Crisp, 209
olives
  black
    Vegetable Stuffed
      Peppers, 162
onion soup mix
  Meatloaf, 144
orange juice
  Overnight French Toast, 31
  Paradise Island Chicken,
    102
oregano
  Best Bean and Ham Soup,
    54
  Carnitas, 122
  Chicken Cacciatore, 91

Chicken Noodle Soup, 43
Kielbasa Soup, 56
Lemon Sweet Pork Chops,
  127
Meat Sauce for Spaghetti,
  153
Potato and Corn Chowder,
  81
Shrimp Marinara, 165
Super Healthy Cabbage
  Soup, 76
Turkey Lasagna, 110
Veggie Minestrone, 75
Walking Tacos, 148
White Chicken Chili, 49
Overnight French Toast, 31
Overnight Mexican Breakfast
  Casserole, 26
Overnight Oat Groats, 35
Overnight Steel Cut Oatmeal,
  34

P
paprika
  Barbecued Pork Chops, 128
  Chuck Roast, 136
  Sausage, Carrots, Potatoes
    and Cabbage, 130
  Spicy Black Bean Sweet
    Potato Stew, 78
Paprika Pork Chops and Rice,
  129
Paradise Island Chicken, 102
parsley
  Bacon Ranch Red Potatoes,
    185
  Beef Mushroom Barley
    Soup, 66
  Beef Vegetable Soup, 65
  Best Bean and Ham Soup,
    54
  Chicken and Corn Soup, 44
  Chicken Marsala, 96
  Glazed Carrots, 170
  Honey Lemon Garlic
    Salmon, 163

Italian Sausage and Sweet
  Pepper Hash, 30
Mediterranean Lentil Soup,
  77
Shrimp Marinara, 165
Simple Lemon Garlic
  Chicken, 92
Peach Crisp, 209
peas
  Chicken Noodle Soup, 43
  split
    Split Pea Soup, 58
  Tuna Noodle Casserole, 166
pie
  Crockery Apple Pie, 210
pie filling
  blueberry
    Blueberry Swirl Dump
      Cake, 201
  cherry
    Cherry Cheesecake, 204
    Cherry Pie Crisp, 206
pizza
  Turkey Slow-Cooker Pizza,
    111
poblano pepper
  Breakfast Burrito Casserole,
    24
popcorn
  Caramel Corn, 193
pork
  butt roast
    Savory Pork Roast, 117
  chops
    Barbecued Pork Chops,
      128
    Lemon Sweet Pork
      Chops, 127
    Paprika Pork Chops and
      Rice, 129
  loin
    Salsa Verde Pork, 121
  roast
    Cranberry Jalapeño Pork
      Roast, 125

Simple Shredded Pork Tacos, 124
shoulder butt roast
 Italian Shredded Pork Stew, 53
shoulder roast
 BBQ Pork Sandwiches, 118
 Carnitas, 122
pork and beans
 Ranch Beans, 186
Pork Baby Back Ribs, 115
Potato and Corn Chowder, 81
Potato-Bacon Gratin, 29
potatoes
 Asparagus Bake, 178
 Beef Stew, 68
 Beef Vegetable Soup, 65
 Best Smashed Potatoes, 182
 Breakfast Burrito Casserole, 24
 Breakfast for Dinner Casserole, 23
 Chicken and Corn Soup, 44
 Coca-Cola Roast, 135
 Creamy Potato Chowder, 61
 hash browns
  Breakfast for Dinner Casserole, 23
  Fiesta Hashbrowns, 27
  Lightened-Up Cheesy Potatoes, 183
 Italian Sausage and Sweet Pepper Hash, 30
 Kelly's Company Omelette, 19
 Kielbasa Soup, 56
 Overnight Mexican Breakfast Casserole, 26
 red
  Bacon Ranch Red Potatoes, 185
  Chicken Stew, 48
  Potato and Corn Chowder, 81
  Sausage, Carrots, Potatoes and Cabbage, 130
 sweet
  Italian Shredded Pork Stew, 53
  Spicy Black Bean Sweet Potato Stew, 78
 tater tots
  Breakfast for Dinner Casserole, 23
potato flakes
 Best Bean and Ham Soup, 54
Potato Soup, 59
Potluck Baked Corn, 172
poultry seasoning
 Chicken and Dumplings, 104
 Traditional Turkey Breast, 109
protein powder
 vanilla
  Overnight Oat Groats, 35
pudding
 Best Bread Pudding, 198
 Chocolate Pudding Cake, 203
 Coconut Rice Pudding, 211, 212
 S'mores Lava Cake, 202

Q

quiche
 Easy Quiche, 16
Quick-'N'-Easy Meat-Free Lasagna, 159
Quinoa and Black Beans, 187

R

Ranch Beans, 186
ranch dressing mix
 Bacon Ranch Red Potatoes, 185
 Salsa Ranch Chicken with Black Beans, 106
ravioli
 Cheese Ravioli Casserole, 158

red pepper flakes
 Green Beans with Bacon, 174
 Walking Tacos, 148
ribs
 Easiest Ever BBQ Country Ribs, 116
 Pork Baby Back Ribs, 115
rice
 arborio
  Coconut Rice Pudding, 211
 brown
  Paprika Pork Chops and Rice, 129
 Coconut Rice Pudding, 212
 Stuffed Green Peppers, 146
 Vegetable Stuffed Peppers, 162
 wild
  Steak and Rice Dinner, 143
rosemary
 Flavorful French Dip, 138
 Kelly's Company Omelette, 19
 Savory Pork Roast, 117
 Winter Squash with Herbs and Butter, 180
Rosemary Carrots, 169

S

salmon
 Honey Lemon Garlic Salmon, 163
salsa
 Black Bean Soup with Chicken and Salsa, 46
 Breakfast Burrito Casserole, 24
 Chipotle Beef Chili, 72
 Easy Chicken Tortilla Soup, 45
 Salsa Lime Chicken, 92
 Salsa Verde Pork, 121
 Three Bean Chili, 84

Salsa Lime Chicken, 92
Salsa Ranch Chicken with
   Black Beans, 106
Salsa Verde Pork, 121
sausage
  breakfast
    Breakfast for Dinner
      Casserole, 23
  chorizo
    Breakfast Burrito
      Casserole, 24
    Easy Quiche, 16
    Kelly's Company Omelette,
      19
  kielbasa
    Kielbasa Soup, 56
  smoked
    Sausage, Carrots, Potatoes
      and Cabbage, 130
  spicy
    Overnight Mexican
      Breakfast Casserole, 26
  turkey
    Fiesta Hashbrowns, 27
    Italian Sausage and Sweet
      Pepper Hash, 30
    Sloppy Joes, 149
Sausage, Carrots, Potatoes and
   Cabbage, 130
Savory Pork Roast, 117
Shrimp Marinara, 165
Simple Lemon Garlic
   Chicken, 92
Simple Shredded Pork Tacos,
   124
Six-Can Soup, 80
Sloppy Joes, 149
slow cooker
  Apple Cinnamon Oatmeal,
    38
  Apple Crisp, 207
  Asparagus Bake, 178
  Balsamic Chicken, 98
  Banana Chocolate Chip
    Bars, 194
  Barbecued Chicken, 99

Barbecued Pork Chops, 128
Beef Stew, 68
Beef with Broccoli, 141
Best Bread Pudding, 198
Best Smashed Potatoes, 182
Black Bean Chili, 85
Black Bean Soup with
   Chicken and Salsa, 46
Blueberry Swirl Dump
   Cake, 201
Carnitas, 122
Cheese Ravioli Casserole,
   158
Cherry Cheesecake, 204
Cherry Pie Crisp, 206
Chicken and Corn Soup, 44
Chicken Cacciatore, 91
Chicken Dijon Dinner, 101
Chicken Marsala, 96
Chipotle Beef Chili, 72
Chocolate Pudding Cake,
   203
Chuck Roast, 136
Coca-Cola Roast, 135
Coconut Rice Pudding, 211
Convenient Slow-Cooker
   Lasagna, 151
Cranberry Jalapeño Pork
   Roast, 125
Cream of Broccoli and
   Mushroom Soup, 83
Creamy Italian Chicken,
   103
Creamy Potato Chowder, 61
Crockery Apple Pie, 210
Easiest Ever BBQ Country
   Ribs, 116
Easy Chicken Tortilla Soup,
   45
Easy Enchilada Shredded
   Chicken, 107
Fiesta Hashbrowns, 27
Flavorful French Dip, 138
German Chocolate
   Oatmeal, 37
Glazed Carrots, 170

Gooey Cookie Dessert, 196
Goulash, 145
Green Beans Caesar, 175
Ham and Bean Stew, 55
Italian Sausage and Sweet
   Pepper Hash, 30
Italian Shredded Pork Stew,
   53
Kelly's Company Omelette,
   19
Kielbasa Soup, 56
Lemon Sweet Pork Chops,
   127
Lightened-Up Cheesy
   Potatoes, 183
Meat Sauce for Spaghetti,
   153
Mediterranean Lentil Soup,
   77
Overnight French Toast, 31
Overnight Mexican
   Breakfast Casserole, 26
Overnight Oat Groats, 35
Overnight Steel-Cut
   Oatmeal, 34
Paradise Island Chicken,
   102
Peach Crisp, 209
Potato and Corn Chowder,
   81
Potluck Baked Corn, 172
Quick-'N'-Easy Meat-Free
   Lasagna, 159
Quinoa and Black Beans,
   187
Ranch Beans, 186
Rosemary Carrots, 169
Salsa Ranch Chicken with
   Black Beans, 106
Salsa Verde Pork, 121
Savory Pork Roast, 117
Shrimp Marinara, 165
Simple Lemon Garlic
   Chicken, 92
Simple Shredded Pork
   Tacos, 124

Six-Can Soup, 80
Sloppy Joes, 149
S'mores Lava Cake, 202
Split Pea Soup, 58
Steak and Rice Dinner, 143
Stuffed Green Peppers, 146
Tortellini with Broccoli, 157
Turkey Lasagna, 110
Turkey Slow-Cooker Pizza, 111
Tuscan Beef Stew, 69
Vegetable Stuffed Peppers, 162
White Chicken Chili, 49
Winter Squash with Herbs and Butter, 180
S'mores Lava Cake, 202
soup
   Beef Mushroom Barley Soup, 66
   Beef Vegetable Soup, 65
   Best Bean and Ham Soup, 54
   Chicken and Corn Soup, 44
   Chicken Noodle Soup, 43
   Cream of Broccoli and Mushroom Soup, 83
   Creamy Potato Chowder, 61
   Easy Chicken Tortilla Soup, 45
   Kielbasa Soup, 56
   Mediterranean Lentil Soup, 77
   Potato and Corn Chowder, 81
   Potato Soup, 59
   Six-Can Soup, 80
   Split Pea Soup, 58
   Super Healthy Cabbage Soup, 76
   Veggie Minestrone, 75
sour cream
   Salsa Ranch Chicken with Black Beans, 106
Southwestern Egg Casserole, 20

soy sauce
   Beef with Broccoli, 141
   Chicken Dijon Dinner, 101
   Paradise Island Chicken, 102
   Vegetable Stuffed Peppers, 162
Spaghetti and Meatballs, 152
Spicy Black Bean Sweet Potato Stew, 78
spinach
   Egg Bites, 15
   Potato-Bacon Gratin, 29
   Veggie Minestrone, 75
Split Pea Soup, 58
squash
   Winter Squash with Herbs and Butter, 180
Steak and Rice Dinner, 143
stew
   Beef Stew, 68
   Chicken Stew, 48
   Ham and Bean Stew, 55
   Italian Shredded Pork Stew, 53
   Spicy Black Bean Sweet Potato Stew, 78
   Tuscan Beef Stew, 69
Strawberry Shortcake, 199
Stuffed Green Peppers, 146
Super Healthy Cabbage Soup, 76

T

taco seasoning
   Goulash, 145
   Salsa Ranch Chicken with Black Beans, 106
tapioca
   Beef Stew, 68
   Fiesta Hashbrowns, 27
tarragon
   Chili Comerford-Style, 71
   Kelly's Company Omelette, 19
   Winter Squash with Herbs and Butter, 180

Three Bean Chili, 84
thyme
   Beef Mushroom Barley Soup, 66
   Chicken Noodle Soup, 43
   Cream of Broccoli and Mushroom Soup, 83
   Flavorful French Dip, 138
   Italian Sausage and Sweet Pepper Hash, 30
   Kelly's Company Omelette, 19
   Kielbasa Soup, 56
   Mediterranean Lentil Soup, 77
   Potato and Corn Chowder, 81
   Winter Squash with Herbs and Butter, 180
tomatoes
   Balsamic Chicken, 98
   Beef Vegetable Soup, 65
   Black Bean Chili, 85
   Chicken Cacciatore, 91
   Chili Comerford-Style, 71
   Easy Enchilada Shredded Chicken, 107
   Goulash, 145
   Meatless Ziti, 160
   Meat Sauce for Spaghetti, 153
   Mediterranean Lentil Soup, 77
   Paprika Pork Chops and Rice, 129
   Salsa Verde Pork, 121
   Shrimp Marinara, 165
   Six-Can Soup, 80
   Spaghetti and Meatballs, 152
   Spicy Black Bean Sweet Potato Stew, 78
   stewed
      Easy Chicken Tortilla Soup, 45
      Super Healthy Cabbage Soup, 76

Three Bean Chili, 84
Tuscan Beef Stew, 69
Vegetable Stuffed Peppers, 162
Veggie Minestrone, 75
tomato juice
   Beef Stew, 68
   Super Healthy Cabbage Soup, 76
tomato paste
   Kielbasa Soup, 56
   Meat Sauce for Spaghetti, 153
   Shrimp Marinara, 165
   Turkey Lasagna, 110
   Vegetable Stuffed Peppers, 162
tomato sauce
   Black Bean Chili, 85
   Cheese Ravioli Casserole, 158
   Chicken and Corn Soup, 44
   Chicken Cacciatore, 91
   Convenient Slow-Cooker Lasagna, 151
   Easy Chicken Tortilla Soup, 45
   Goulash, 145
   Meat Sauce for Spaghetti, 153
   Quick-'N'-Easy Meat-Free Lasagna, 159
   Sloppy Joes, 149
   Spaghetti and Meatballs, 152
   Stuffed Green Peppers, 146
   Turkey Slow-Cooker Pizza, 111
tomato soup
   Barbecued Chicken, 99
   Six-Can Soup, 80
   Tuscan Beef Stew, 69
Tortellini with Broccoli, 157
tortilla chips
   Easy Chicken Tortilla Soup, 45

tortillas
   Breakfast Burrito Casserole, 24
   Carnitas, 122
Traditional Turkey Breast, 109
Tuna Noodle Casserole, 166
turkey
   breast
      Traditional Turkey Breast, 109
   ground, 153
      Turkey Lasagna, 110
      Turkey Slow-Cooker Pizza, 111
   sausage
      Fiesta Hashbrowns, 27
      Italian Sausage and Sweet Pepper Hash, 30
      Sloppy Joes, 149
Turkey Lasagna, 110
Turkey Slow-Cooker Pizza, 111
Tuscan Beef Stew, 69

V

Vegetable Stuffed Peppers, 162
Veggie Minestrone, 75
vinegar
   apple cider
      Chuck Roast, 136
      Pork Baby Back Ribs, 115
      Sloppy Joes, 149
   balsamic
      Balsamic Chicken, 98
   Barbecued Chicken, 99
   Barbecued Pork Chops, 128
   cider
      Ham and Bean Stew, 55
   red wine
      Green Beans Caesar, 175
   white wine
      Chicken Dijon Dinner, 101

W

Walking Tacos, 148
White Chicken Chili, 49

wine
   red
      Tuscan Beef Stew, 69
   white
      Salsa Verde Pork, 121
Winter Squash with Herbs and Butter, 180
Worcestershire sauce
   Barbecued Brisket, 137
   Barbecued Chicken, 99
   Barbecued Pork Chops, 128
   Sloppy Joes, 149

Y

yogurt
   Greek
      Best Smashed Potatoes, 182
      Lightened-Up Cheesy Potatoes, 183

Z

ziti
   Meatless Ziti, 160

About the Author

Hope Comerford is a mom, wife, elementary music teacher, blogger, recipe developer, public speaker, Young Living Essential Oils essential oil enthusiast/educator, and published author. In 2013, she was diagnosed with a severe gluten intolerance and since then has spent many hours creating easy, practical, and delicious gluten-free recipes that can be enjoyed by both those who are affected by gluten and those who are not.

Growing up, Hope spent many hours in the kitchen with her Meme (grandmother) and her love for cooking grew from there. While working on her master's degree when her daughter was young, Hope turned to her slow cookers for some salvation and sanity. It was from there she began truly experimenting with recipes and quickly learned she had the ability to get a little more creative in the kitchen and develop her own recipes.

In 2010, Hope started her blog, *A Busy Mom's Slow Cooker Adventures*, to simply share the recipes she was making with her family and friends. She never imagined people all over the world would begin visiting her page and sharing her recipes with others as well. In 2013, Hope self-published her first cookbook, *Slow Cooker Recipes 10 Ingredients or Less and Gluten-Free*, and then later wrote *The Gluten-Free Slow Cooker*.

Hope became the new brand ambassador and author of Fix-It and Forget-It in mid-2016. Since then, she has brought her excitement and creativeness to the Fix-It and Forget-It brand. Through Fix-It and Forget-It, she has written *Fix-It and Forget-It Healthy One-Pot Meals Cookbook*, *Fix-It and Forget-It Slow Cooker Freezer Meals Cookbook*, *Fix-It and Forget-It Freezer to Instant Pot Cookbook*, *Welcome Home 30-Minute Meals*, *Fix-It and Forget-It Weeknight Favorites Cookbook*, and many more.

Hope lives in the city of Clinton Township, Michigan, near Metro Detroit. She has been happily married to her husband and best friend, Justin, since 2008. Together they have two children, Ella and Gavin, who are her motivation, inspiration, and heart. In her spare time, Hope enjoys traveling, singing, cooking, reading books, working on wooden puzzles, spending time with friends and family, and relaxing.